D0946204

Kate Leaver is an author and journalist for *The Guardian*, *The Telegraph*, *Vogue* and *Future Women*, among others. She lives between Sydney and London with her boyfriend, Jono, and their dog, Bertie. You can find her on Twitter and Instagram @kateileaver.

GOOD DOG

GOOD DOG

KATE LEAVER

HarperCollins*Publishers*

HarperCollins*Publishers*

First published in Australia in 2020
by HarperCollins*Publishers* Australia Pty Limited
ABN 36 009 913 517
harpercollins.com.au

Copyright © Kate Leaver 2020

The right of Kate Leaver to be identified as the author of this work has been asserted by her in accordance with the *Copyright Amendment (Moral Rights) Act 2000.*

This work is copyright. Apart from any use as permitted under the *Copyright Act 1968*, no part may be reproduced, copied, scanned, stored in a retrieval system, recorded, or transmitted, in any form or by any means, without the prior written permission of the publisher.

HarperCollins*Publishers*
Level 13, 201 Elizabeth Street, Sydney NSW 2000, Australia
Unit D1, 63 Apollo Drive, Rosedale, Auckland 0632, New Zealand
A 53, Sector 57, Noida, UP, India
1 London Bridge Street, London, SE1 9GF, United Kingdom
Bay Adelaide Centre, East Tower, 22 Adelaide Street West, 41st floor, Toronto, Ontario M5H 4E3, Canada
195 Broadway, New York NY 10007, USA

A catalogue record for this book is available from the National Library of Australia

ISBN 978 1 4607 5889 2 (paperback)
ISBN 978 1 4607 1262 7 (ebook)

Cover design by Darren Holt, HarperCollins Design Studio
Front cover image by Stephanie Reis/Getty Images
Typeset in Sabon LT Std by Kirby Jones
Line drawings by Laura New
Photograph of Kate Leaver and Bertie (on back cover and on page 277) by Jenny Lewis
Printed and bound in Australia by McPherson's Printing Group
The papers used by HarperCollins in the manufacture of this book are a natural, recyclable product made from wood grown in sustainable plantation forests. The fibre source and manufacturing processes meet recognised international environmental standards, and carry certification.

To my grandma Lyn James, the only person I've ever known who loved dogs as much as I do.

Contents

INTRODUCTION

For the love of dog

'SHALL WE BRING OUR firstborn son with us?'

'Don't call him that. He's a dog.'

'But I love him like he is my child. He's my hairy, grubby little child.'

I get in trouble with my boyfriend whenever I refer to our dog, Bertie, as my firstborn son. The anthropomorphism is a bit much, even for him, who otherwise adores our small, smelly companion as much as I do. I can't find another way of conveying how serious I am about my affection for our 58-centimetre-long hairy housemate. He is a living creature, roughly the size of a big new-born human, who depends on us for food and love and warmth and safety. The way he nuzzles his wet nose into my neck while we watch telly at night makes me feel maternal. I'm not a mother, so this is the most powerfully responsible I've ever felt for a breathing, snuffling, snoring, farting being. Besides, I find it funny to wind my boyfriend up.

I'm not entirely mad, though. Every time I whisper 'Who's my baby boy?' into my dog's floppy, silver-tipped ears, I am simply verbalising a complex bond between two species that has existed for tens of thousands of years. The remains of a dog from 14,000 years ago were found buried beside a family of humans in Germany; a proximity in death that implies a life lived together. Archaeologists have found dog bones that were buried lovingly beside humans in Siberia 8,000 years ago, and North America 9,000 years ago. Chemical analysis has revealed that these dogs ate the same food as their accompanying humans, meaning they were well cared for and fed. They were treated, in some ways, as equals. Human beings used to kill and eat dogs, too, but in most cultures that stopped once people started treating dogs as beloved companions, status symbols, working dogs and members of the family. With protection from human beings, dogs have been substantially more evolutionarily successful than their original ancestor, the Eurasian grey wolf. It's less about survival of the fittest, more about survival of the cutest.

Experts squabble over exactly what prompted wolves to evolve into human-friendly dogs. Some say that humans enlisted wolves to hunt for them, but actually wolves are not the kind of species to give up food once they have chased it down. It's more likely that a very long time ago — somewhere between 14,000 and 33,000 years ago, according to feuding scientists — wolves started following packs of humans, probably hoping to pick up a few food scraps. Humans recognised the wolves' potential usefulness as hunters and guardians, so they learned to work together as a team and then share the food. They would also have relied on these companion wolves/ prototype dogs to warn them of danger, too, by barking at any strangers, intruders or unwelcome beasts who approached their tribe's home. Archaeological evidence tells us that when humans migrated across the planet, they took their canine pals with them. The friendlier among these wolves became true companions, protected and treated with affection. Friendly wolves bred with friendly wolves, which ultimately resulted in the dog, a slightly genetically different creature.

These creatures started evolving alongside us, getting closer to the cuties we coddle these days. Gradually, their ears got floppier, their tails got waggier and their coats became splotchy. The closeness between dogs and our ancestors even affected the way their brains developed — and possibly ours. Some scientists argue that we humans have a diminished sense of smell because we have formed such a close bond with dogs, who can do some of our sniffing for us. Meanwhile, dogs have learned to widen their eyes and behave adorably to catch and then keep our attention. Putting on their cutest possible facial expression increases their chance of survival, getting affection and delicious treats. Over centuries, we have forged a symbiotic relationship with our canine friends, exchanging protection, affection and companionship.

While dogs certainly used to help us track down other beasts for mealtimes, a crucial part of their appeal has always been their cuteness. I'm not the only one who's had her parenting instinct triggered by a puppy; human beings have long doted on dogs in a pseudo-parental sort of way. It's why our ancestors held burial rituals for them. It's why they brought dogs along with them when they moved homes. It's why experiments have demonstrated that we have more empathy for puppies and dogs than we do for adult human beings. It's why, ultimately, the term 'fur baby' exists, even though I refrain from using it myself.

The next time I need to justify my intense affection for my dog, perhaps I should present my boyfriend with a study undertaken in 2015 at Azabu University in Japan. Takefumi Kikusui, from the Department of Animal Science and

Biotechnology, got together with his colleagues to investigate why we are so close to our pets. He had been a dog owner for 15 years and, just like me, wondered at the intensity of the human–dog bond. To find out more about what happens when we interact with our dogs, he invited 30 people to bring their dogs into the laboratory. He also took part, with his two standard poodles, Anita and Jasmine. For comparison, he invited a few people who had tried to domesticate wolves and he also invited their wolves.

Upon arrival, they were all — humans, dogs and wolves — asked to provide a urine sample. Researchers took away these urine samples for analysis, and then asked each person to play with their dog or wolf for 30 minutes. They hung out in a room with their beloved pups, most making eye contact with their pups for minutes at a time. The wolves, as you can imagine, didn't partake in a lot of loving eye contact. After half an hour, another urine sample was taken, which was then tested, looking for any spike in oxytocin levels compared with the first sample.

Oxytocin is known as the cuddle hormone, for its calming qualities. It makes us feel happy, safe and loved. We tend to get a surge of it when we touch other human beings, and it is an important way we learn to bond and trust. After the half-hour of playing, cuddling and sustained eye contact, the dogs had a 130 per cent increase in oxytocin levels. The dog owners, both male and female, experienced a 300 per cent increase. There was no such result for the owners of the wolves, or for people who didn't make much eye contact with their dogs. The researchers concluded that making eye contact with our dogs produces oxytocin, which gives us that lovely, warm feeling of calm and happiness.

This reaction happens with parents and their human babies, too. When a mother or father holds their child in their arms and gazes into their eyes, there's a feedback loop of oxytocin between them that powerfully bonds them. An exchange of oxytocin is hugely important in building trust, sympathy and affection between human beings. It is one of the most important factors in human babies forming an attachment to their parents, the strength of which can determine their emotional openness and resilience for a lifetime.

These researchers say a similar thing happens when we look at our dogs, which goes some way to explaining my maternal feelings. Certainly, when I stare into my dog's wonky eyes — one of which is always wandering off to the side — I feel happy and calm. It makes me feel closer to him. Does it make me feel like he could be a child substitute? Perhaps.

Other research suggests that patting our dogs also produces oxytocin, which is why stroking my dog's ears and scratching him under the chin is such a healing activity for me. It also gives him a dose of oxytocin, which makes him sleepy and content and well behaved. It makes him love me right back, if we're to believe that dogs are capable of that sort of feeling, which I absolutely do. This lovely exchange of oxytocin may have been integral in the domestication of dogs in the first place, scientists say. It is appealing and beneficial for both humans and dogs, explaining why we kept gravitating towards each other.

The dog–human bond is probably the most extraordinary cross-species relationship on the planet, although cat people may of course object. We are able to get so close to these waggly, slobbery creatures partly because we understand each other. You may not think you speak fluent dog, but actually we are all fairly good at reading a dog's expressions. We know an aggressive bark from a playful one, and a growl from a squeal of pain. We know that their tap-dance at the door means they're happy to see us. We can tell when a dog is hungry, frustrated, angry, scared, excited and sleepy. They give us cues in their body language and with the noises they make, so we can try to understand what they need from us. Similarly, dogs know the difference between being praised and getting in trouble. They can differentiate between tones of human voice and even learn certain words, such as their own names and things like 'walk' or 'sit' or 'dinner'.

We communicate more clearly and comprehensively with dogs than we do with just about any other species. Just think: would you know if a duck was sad? Could you tell if a lizard was was happy to see you? Could you train a fish to fetch things for you? We have learned to speak dog, and dogs, in turn, have found a way to understand us. Their ability to interpret human gestures is extraordinary, especially when you consider that our much closer relatives, chimpanzees and bonobos, cannot do so nearly as well. Dogs can also be effectively trained using visual cues, scent and treats. They are repeatedly proving that they understand us better than any other species.

Beyond linguistic understanding, we now believe that dogs can pick up on our moods and our emotions. Canine experts say that our pet dogs are so in tune with us that we can actually shape their personalities and affect what kind of dog they will grow up to be. Often, they reflect our own temperament back to us, mimicking our calm or our anxieties. Dogs are perhaps more emotionally intelligent and alert than we expect, although of course I am not at all surprised to hear that mine might be sentimentally sophisticated.

They can give us profound emotional support. Consider this fantastic 2009 study led by academic Lawrence A Kurdek at Wright State University. Researchers spoke to 975 dog owners and found that, in times of stress, people were more likely to turn to their dogs for comfort than to their parents, siblings or children. They make exceptional companions for this reason, but they're also perfect as service animals. This has seen a rapidly growing number of dogs now being trained as assistance and therapy dogs. They've been known to smell cancer in patients. They can detect a diabetic person's blood sugar levels. They help nervous children read. They soothe children who live with autism. They help people who live with blindness and deafness navigate the world. They tend to people who live with mental illnesses. They help people with dementia to remember, even if it's only for a moment. They work in our armed forces, with our veterans, on our police forces and in our prisons. They play integral parts in therapy and rehabilitation programs the world over.

Dogs improve our lives in myriad important, fascinating ways. Our centuries-long, enduring relationship with these creatures is always evolving, as we learn more ways to be useful and close to one another. Now, more than ever, we can see the clear health benefits of living with a dog by our side. We are training them to help and support us in more ways than our ancestors could probably have imagined — and hopefully giving them a life of safety, warmth, treats and belly scratches in return.

Research has shown that dogs are extremely good for our health, both physical and mental. Studies suggest that children who grow up in households with dogs develop better immune systems and get sick less often. They're also potentially more empathetic, as they learn to be gentle and exchange love with a living creature. The health benefits of dog companionship extend into adulthood, too. On average, dog owners have lower levels of anxiety, lower blood pressure, lower cholesterol levels and fewer heart attacks than those who live without a dog. They tend to be more physically active than the dogless, simply because they get into the routine of taking their beloved companion for walks.

Dogs are also extremely good for our social lives, in part because they make us more approachable in public. Dog people talk to dog people at the park, which can lead to small moments of connection. People delight in seeing dogs out and about, and frequently chat to the person at the end of their lead. Thanks to dogs' friendship, oxytocin-boosting snuggles and elated greeting when we arrive home, people who live with dogs tend to respond better to stress.

That's what this book is about: the remarkable health benefits of keeping a dog as a companion. It's about a uniquely wonderful relationship between two species that has endured for thousands of years. It's about a new phase in that affiliation; a phase in which we teach our companions to provide us with vital healthcare and emotional support. It's for anyone who has loved a dog and known their love in return.

I felt that I needed to write this book, mostly out of respect for Bertie. I felt that people ought to know what a fiercely cute but also enormously helpful creature he is. Since he came into my life, he's been the most generous, transformative little munchkin and I am thankful for his every snuffling, snorting breath.

Just months into having him, I started thinking about how extraordinary our pets can be, particularly when we need extra support or even, perhaps, a reason to keep living. My last book, *The Friendship Cure*, was about the importance of friendship and the scourge of loneliness. This book is really an extension of that idea, only it's specifically about the remarkable companionship we can expect from animals — in particular, dogs. Once I started thinking about the extreme loveliness of dogs, I couldn't stop. I was convinced that I could find other examples of dogs who had changed and indeed saved people's lives. I set out to find other stories, to make my case for the profound importance of dogs. My research led me to meet ten of the most wonderful creatures — big and small, gentle and lively. I travelled across the world to hear about how they've helped people with their mental and physical health problems. I've spent time with some of the most effusive dog people I've ever met and it was an absolute joy. I cannot think of a lovelier research topic and I feel so lucky to have patted to many cuties and got away with calling it work.

And so, I want to introduce you to those magnificent pups I've met over the past year. Over the course of this book, I think you'll come to agree with me that dogs are unrivalled in their contribution to human lives. You'll see that, across all age groups and life stages, they have the capacity to improve a person's existence.

First, you'll meet my beloved shih tzu, Bertie. Since my boyfriend and I adopted him, he has become the third member of our family. I spend more time with Bertie than any other living creature, and I am grateful every day to have him by my side. I live with bipolar disorder and still quite regularly plummet into depression. During these episodes, when I'm chemically bereft, Bertie refuses to leave my side. His warm, hairy little body next to mine reminds me why it's worth staying alive. He gets me out of the house each morning, when otherwise I could stay in my pyjamas for weeks. He is my solace on painfully melancholy days, and my absolute joy on the days I am able to feel it.

After reading about my Bert, you'll hear about a darling, near-elderly, mostly-deaf pug named Missy. She had a rough start in life, being kept outside and forced to produce many puppies in less-than-perfect conditions. When she met 11-year-old Cody, she really landed on her funny, black-socked feet. She helped him live more easily with himself and his autism diagnosis. He helped her settle into a loving family, in a safe, warm home. May she escort Cody into his teenage years as safely and as sweetly as possible.

Next, you'll meet trained therapy dog Echo: a sturdy, sprightly labrador the colour of night. He lives with primary-school teacher Aideen, who takes him into work with her each day. Children come to sit with Echo — sometimes they read to him or do their homework by his side. Sometimes they confide in him something that they are not quite ready to share with adult human beings just yet. He helps primary-school kids with their literacy levels, but also with their grief and anguish and insecurity. He knows that when he's got his harness on, it's time to be patient and earnest and good.

After Echo, you'll meet valiant border collie Pip, who knows how to detect when the blood sugar levels of her owner, Katie, change. Pip sleeps by Katie at night, and rushes to wake her parents if her young owner's blood sugar levels get too low or too high, allowing interventions that have saved Katie's life numerous times. Pip and Katie are a remarkable pair — resilient and clever and kind. Then, you'll meet Jingles, who works in a prison. You will hear from a young man in Northern Ireland known as 'wee Barry' whose life has been touched by an energetic, four-legged friend. Jingles is really just at the beginning of his career and I expect he will help countless other inmates in his time, not to mention the staff and his family.

Next, along comes gorgeous guide dog Poppi. She belongs to Liz, who has a degenerative eye condition that means she cannot see well. Together, they can navigate the world safely, happily, steadily and at a reasonable pace. The money to raise and train Poppi was left as a bequest by a wonderfully generous couple who just wanted to change one person's life. That person was Liz — and how lucky Poppi and Liz are to have one another. Speaking of luck, it was extremely lucky that

Mya, our next dog, met her person, too. Mark is a war veteran who developed PTSD after his service. He didn't ask for help for many years and, when he finally did, it came in the form of a puppy who could fit in his hands. Mya has saved Mark's life twice, by stopping him from hurting himself. They keep each other safe and content.

After Mya, we meet Gwen. A sweet, blonde labrador with special training, Gwen works in court with a volunteer therapy dog handler called Julie. Together, they meet and console victims and witnesses who have to testify, many of whom have been affected by sexual violence. Theirs is an important job, and they do it beautifully. I only hope programs like theirs will become better funded and more widespread over the years, so more people have the chance to access them. Then, we meet Jack. Or should I say, Sir Jack Spratticus. He's a wily border terrier who lives with a woman called Vanessa. Ness, as she's known, has had a hard life. She was abused as a child and teenager, and now she lives with dissociate identity disorder, among other things. She has trained Sir Jack to fetch her medication, bring her the landline phone and comfort her through panic attacks. Sir Jack is Ness's reason for being.

After that, we visit a schnoodle by the name of Teddy — Ted, once you get to know him. He is the beloved companion of a man named Andy. Ted actually woke Andy from a coma and helped nurse him back to health. Now, he works at the same hospital as a therapy dog, greeting and comforting sick people, many of whom have suffered from strokes. In the time since we met, Andy lost someone very close to him and he says Teddy was the most enormous comfort throughout.

Finally, we'll meet another schnoodle, called Noodle, who accompanies her human, Debbie, to dementia wards. She helps elderly people remember, even for a moment, who they might have been. She snuggles, licks and nuzzles people who crave affection.

It is my absolute delight to have met all of these very good boys and girls. I hope you will come to love them, too. They are crucially important to their human companions, just as Bertie is to me. If you've ever known the true friendship of a dog, particularly at a time when you truly needed it, then you might recognise your own luck and affection in these stories. Dogs can be our greatest allies, our sweetest helpers and, indeed, our best friends. They give us solace, warmth, comfort and joy. They make us so besotted with them that we think of them as members of our families. Personally, I wouldn't have it any other way.

CHAPTER 1

Bertie, the dog who saved me from myself

IT'S EASY TO BE cynical about love at first sight.

Until you're home alone one Friday night and you see pictures of a small, scruffy dog on the internet and he has soft paws and wonky eyes and a pink tongue and all of a sudden you just know that your life will never be complete until he's in your arms.

When that kind of love came for me, I was lying on the sofa in my pyjamas. My main hobby at the time was scrolling through pet adoption sites. I'd stared into a lot of dog faces, but as soon as I saw this one particular face I knew immediately: he's ours. I knew with the kind of certainty we traditionally reserve for making eye contact with handsome strangers across rooms at parties. I just knew.

I'd spent months searching for the right creature for my boyfriend and me to adopt. One day we nearly brought home an obese springer spaniel called Fat Scotty because his majestic, plump face was irresistible. Unfortunately, he had a tendency to strain against the lead with all 48 of his kilos, and nearly pulled me face-first into the mud. I simply couldn't handle him — and so he was likely rehomed to someone with stronger biceps. We needed someone smaller. Someone gentler. Someone with an almost flat face, a completely undignified beard, and a disproportionately long body. Someone whose little paws make *tap-tap* sounds on wooden floorboards, who snores like a beast three times his size. A shih tzu. A shih tzu was what we needed; I knew it in my heart.

As it happens, I'd rescued a shih tzu before: an elderly lass with crooked, rotting teeth I christened Lady Fluffington (silent middle name: Beyoncé). She was stubborn and funny and haughty, like an old lady who'd earned her crankiness. She snored heartily and farted courageously, all her days. She was six kilos of heaven, with a face only a mother could love — which is lucky, because I thought of myself as her mama for the six years we had her. She slept beside me every night, with my boyfriend at the time relegated to another bed. She would curl up in my arms and make noises you would swear had to come from a larger beast. She came with me just about anywhere she could, sitting buckled into the passenger seat of my blue car, watching out the window in case there was something that required a single, loud bark on our way past.

My then-boyfriend and I rescued Lady Fluff from a place in Sydney called Monika's Doggie Rescue when she was about eight years old. She had a slipped disc, a bad hip and an even worse haircut. In photographs on the website advertising her availability to be adopted, she could be seen wearing a multicoloured cardigan and snarling into the camera with as much casual contempt as she could muster. She had been at Monika's shelter a long time, having been saved from a pound planning to kill her because they couldn't find her a home.

Lady Fluff took her time getting accustomed to living with us, but once she settled in she was the queen of her domain, entitled to every treat and every cuddle she desired. She once stole an entire carrot from the kitchen and devoured it, somehow, with her few remaining teeth and the power of her snapping, pink gums. She was brittle and tender and full of personality. She had opinions, and she made them known with short, sharp, surprisingly arresting barks no matter what time of the day or night it was. I once made the mistake of dressing her in a duck outfit — I've never seen such disdain exuding from a creature before or since. She was a profound treasure. We needed each other — I only wish I had known her earlier in her little life.

I adored Lady Fluffington fiercely and completely. It broke my heart when she died, age 14. She finally expired, many years after she was expected to, in my mother's arms. Dogs sometimes move away from their pack to die, but she simply dragged her fragile body up the bed, laid her head on my mum's shoulder for the last time, exhaled and slipped away. For days, I howled. For months, she was the first thing I thought about in the morning and the last thing I'd picture at night. She was my precious girl and I missed her immediately, viscerally and with a primal sort of anguish that took a long time to recede. I tried looking after other people's dogs to ease the grief, but really I didn't know if I'd ever have the capacity to love another creature like I did that funny little gremlin-lookalike. She was extremely special to me, and I will never forget how heart-achingly good it felt to have her in my arms. RIP, Lady Fluff.

In Lady Fluffington's honour, this time around I scoured the internet for abandoned shih tzus. I was convinced they were uniquely sweet, and I was quietly dead-set on getting another one. So when a small, furry guy called Mungo appeared on the Battersea Dogs and Cats Homes website, I opened his profile with frightening speed. There were four photos of him online, one of which, inexplicably, was of him crouching down to wee on a fence. He was the colour of clotted cream and biscuits, with silver-tipped ears and a black button nose. He had big black eyes that rolled around in their sockets, and an undersupply of teeny white teeth. He wasn't especially handsome; shih tzus tend not to be. Their charm is usually in their defiance and self-assurance, rather than any particular beauty. But oh, he was lovely. Impish and and impossibly sweet.

I was immediately committed to this little mongrel. Already picturing our lives together, picking out toys, dreaming of tiny raincoats ... I already knew, just looking at him, that I could find a way to love him for all his days. My boyfriend, Jono, however, needed some convincing. He'd never owned a dog before and he had this image in his head of the perfect canine companion: sleek, athletic, long-snouted. He wanted a shiny, lithe spaniel — a proper dog who'd bound across country fields and curl up by the fireplace after a hearty run. Not, probably, one whose stumpy legs would carry him only so far between naps. I knew Mungo didn't fit Jono's idea of the perfect dog, but I also knew he'd come to love Mungo if I could just get them to meet.

On this particular evening, my boyfriend was working late. His phone alerted him to 68 WhatsApp messages from me over the course of three hours. First, I sent him a link to Mungo's profile on the rescue site, followed by a slew of messages in which I insisted, in caps-lock, that we go and pick him up immediately. I drew speech bubbles above the dog's head, reading things like *Why won't you love me?* and *Come and get me, Jono*. I made collages of his face. I multiplied the four available photos of him until there were hundreds of his dog face on a page. I sent them all with the desperate perseverance of a child asking her mother for a sweet right after cleaning her teeth: I knew I was being naughty and yet I persisted. Nevertheless, dissatisfied with my efforts up to that point, I printed out Mungo's photos and sticky-taped them inside the bathroom cabinet, underneath the lid of our loo and on our bedroom wall. I slipped A4 print-outs of Mungo's face between our bedsheets and under Jono's pillow. By the time he arrived home later that night, I had successfully conveyed to him that I was completely unravelling in my desperation to have a dog. And not just any dog, though. Mungo.

Out of love, or perhaps defeat, Jono agreed to meet Mungo. In order to get a rescue dog, you typically have to reserve them to indicate your interest and make a time to go in. By this time, it was past opening hours at Battersea Old Windsor, so I sent an after-hours email expressing my keenness to be acquainted with Mungo. We planned to get there in time for opening at ten o'clock the next morning, two trains and a bus away, just down the road from the Queen's residence in Windsor. We arrived early, waited in the car park, and walked in the moment the doors opened. 'We're here to see Mungo,' I said, with joy written all over my face. 'I don't think you are,' said the receptionist. 'A family of four are coming to see him tomorrow.' They had called first thing that morning to reserve Mungo — nobody had checked the email inbox or seen my message from the night before.

I was, as you can imagine, crestfallen. We stumbled outside. I sobbed and collapsed on a bench in the cold. 'It's a rough game,' I howled. Jono quietly comforted me, understanding properly for the first time just how much I love dogs. He would later, obviously, mock me for saying that. And so we went all the way home again, on two trains and a bus. 'But he's our dog,' I kept saying. 'How can they not know he's our dog?'

Back home, without my rascal-faced little mate, I was distraught. I found no solace looking at other dogs on the internet, because I was convinced Mungo was meant to be ours. This is just about the only sort of fate I believe in: dog fate. And so, as stubborn as a shih tzu, I didn't give up hope. Which turned out to be quite correct, because the shelter called the next day to say that the family who'd wanted Mungo couldn't take him home. They already had one dog, and Mungo had snapped at him, displaying precisely the bad temper I'd expected. *Good boy*, I thought. *Wait there, we'll come and get you.*

Jono had a day off work that coming week — it was his birthday and we did have plans, which were promptly cancelled — so we got back on those two trains and a bus. Mungo was brought out to us, wearing a tattered maroon jacket. We took him for a wander around the grounds to see if we got on. I was besotted immediately. He tottered about, leaving paw prints in the snow as he went. We said, 'Yes please, we'll take him home with us immediately, thank you.' So he sat on our laps on two trains and a bus, trembling. He was cold and frightened. Once home, he scrambled about in his new surroundings and immediately began to destroy his new nemesis, a teddy bear we'd bought for him.

We wanted to rename him, and I briefly campaigned for Harry, after Harry Styles and Harry Potter, two of the most important men in my life. Eventually we settled on Gilbert, known to those who love him simply as Bertie. Often just Bert. Sometimes, depending on our mood, any name that can be shortened to Bert will suffice: Herbert, Albert, Robert, Cuthbert, Bertrand ... he's not so fussed about what you call him, just so long as you call.

It wasn't perfect with Bert straight away; it rarely is with dogs. He was nervous in his new home, unsure about us and probably quite scared. He'd been traumatised and he was only nine months old, little mate. The shelter told us he'd been found as a stray and brought in with a gang of other dogs. Actually, many months later we'd find out that might have been wrong. He had been confiscated from a hoarder; someone whose house was dangerously full of things they'd collected, including three neglected shih tzus who had to fight one another for any scraps of food they were given.

By the time he came into the shelter, he was so filthy that the women who welcomed him wrote in his veterinary records that he was grey — although, of course, after a serious bath he was found to be the colour of clotted cream and biscuits, with silver-tipped ears. He had a very bad skin infection, missing or rotting teeth, and furiously matted hair. The angels who worked at the shelter cleaned him up, gave him some medication for his infections, and kept him safe until we could get to him.

Before we came along, he'd had a couple of false starts at a new life: once, with a couple who returned him for being too sprightly, and then the family whose other dog he didn't like. We will never know precisely what Bertie did the first nine months of his life, or quite how poorly treated he was by the people who bought him as a puppy. He's a brave little fellow, though, and it was inevitable that he would have some behavioural issues by the time he first came home with us.

Bert bit me quite badly for at least a month — mostly on the arms and ankles, and once on the left nipple. Then Google taught us to make yelping noises so he would know he was hurting us. He was play-fighting, basically, like he might with a puppy sibling, and he didn't realise that it hurt. Yelping like a pup just let him know that he'd gone too far, and so he learned to be gentler. He drew blood a couple of times first, though. And he howled through the night. He weed on the same corner of our sofa five times in a row, in protest, when we left him. Some days, we weren't sure what we'd done, getting a puppy so young. But I was convinced that all he needed was warmth and attention and love. So that's what we gave him.

It worked, as love often does. Bertie is basically flawless now, if I may say so. He wakes each morning and waits to be let into the bedroom for morning snuggles on the bed. (I cried the first time Jono suggested that Bertie sleep separately to us, but I've come to see the sense in it, so he curls up in a cosy bed just outside our bedroom door.) When we're ready to get up, he goes out for a wee, and then waits by the door while we wipe his paws, one by one. We go for our morning walk in the park each day, where he occasionally growls at dogs and always expects to be greeted by every human we pass. He licks toddlers on their tiny hands and wees a minimum of nine times.

For the rest of the day, Bertie naps at my feet while I write. Occasionally, he stirs to get very angry with one of his toys (usually a beaver we call Brenda), have a bark at the neighbour's cat and clamber onto my lap for some attention, but otherwise he just snoozes. Shih tzus are one of the laziest breeds of dog. Most of them sleep about 16 hours a day. Loves a nap, my boy.

He's also fond of a snuggle. After breakfast, I make myself a coffee and settle on the sofa for a morning Instagram scroll. He rushes over, jumps up and nestles onto my lap for his second round of cuddles for the day. It is the sweetest thing that happens in my life, and I am grateful for it every single day.

Bertie is almost omnipresent in my life; we don't like to be apart. He is my editorial assistant, my best mate and my emotional-support beast. I get separation anxiety when I have to leave him, so he's usually by my side. Jono may be slightly more dignified about it, but he's just as infatuated with Bertie as I am. We dote on him, we text about him throughout every working day and we speak about him on dates. Our romantic nights out now are essentially us swapping anecdotes about Bert, and speculating about what he's doing while we're out of the house (sleeping, it's almost definitely always sleeping).

We have taken thousands of photographs of his ridiculous face, and I post many of them on his personal Instagram. (Bertie's user name is littlebertiethedog and he is technically a 'micro influencer' because he has more than 1,000 followers.) It actually hurts me, sometimes, how much I adore Bert. Looking into his wonky, night-black eyes makes my heart ache. I feel it in my chest, like I'm missing him even though he's right there.

At about four o'clock some mornings, I think about Bert's vulnerability. It's often what I fixate on in those panicky insomniac hours, wondering what I'd do if he got hurt or lost.

I often wonder why we do this to ourselves — love a creature so much that their disappearance would wound us horribly. He has demonstrated profound stupidity in his short life, my precious boy, running off on his own, confronting dogs treble his size, and once leaping through a layer of ice on a frozen pond. I worry that one day he'll be playing at the park and his doggy instinct will tell him to keep running, straight out of our lives. He is incorrigibly dim, in some ways.

Yet he is wonderfully astute in others.

Bert can, for instance, smell depression. I'm convinced that he can. I live with bipolar disorder and still quite regularly plod through depressive episodes, despite being pleasantly medicated. I don't sleep very much, and so I live some days of my life as a spectre of myself, tired and fragile in a way only another insomniac would recognise. When I'm distressed, Bertie can tell. If I ever go back to bed during the day, which I only really do when I'm desperate for respite from the waking world or sad in a way I can't handle while upright, he leaps across our mattress and lays himself across my chest. Often, he lies on my neck. He does not do this at any time when I am happy; it's truly only when I'm upset. It feels like he's trying to protect me, or soothe me. Therapy dogs are actually trained to do precisely this when their humans are in distress. For Bertie, it's instinctive.

Bert's instinct is simply to make as much physical contact with me as possible, to use his body as a buffer between me and the rest of the world. When he's lying on me like that, I can feel his little heart beating against mine and it reminds me what living feels like. He snorts and snuffles and smacks his thick lips together, shifting his long body to find the greatest angle for comfort. I might move him from that position eventually, usually so that I can breathe properly, but he always stays by my side. Refuses to leave me. He lies on his back, with his head in the curve of my armpit, presenting his belly for scratches. He curls into a neat little ball at my feet and snores heartily. He stretches out along the length of my side, with his snout on my shoulder and his hot breath in my ear. He will stay there, until I move.

Some days, when I'm depressed, I just sleep. It's an escape for me; a way of slipping out of my existence for a time without ending it. Often, it's out of my control. It's not really a conscious decision to nap. Sleep simply comes for me, drags me under. It's a heavy sleep, a sleep I can taste on my tongue when I wake, a sleep I can't rouse myself from even if I try. Passing out for hours at a time can be disorienting. So it is an unspeakable comfort to wake beside a small mammal, one whose pink chest rises and falls as he inhales and exhales through wet, hairy nostrils. The warmth of his stout body beside me says, in an instant, that being awake is going to be OK. He makes me feel safe. He makes me feel known. He makes me feel like consciousness is going to be tolerable, for a time.

Together, we sit out the depression. We watch reruns of *Friends* until the most desperate melancholy lifts. We wait out the aching numbness that comes with depression, which is all I'm really capable of doing at those times. I am depleted, but I am not alone. I am not alone. I am not alone. I am never really alone anymore. I always have this precious creature within stroking distance. When I'm counting down the minutes I have left to be awake on a day of depression, waiting for the release of sleep, I pass the time with snuggles. At night and first thing in the morning, I lay my head on Jono's shoulder, wrap my arm across his belly and try to match my breathing to his. I call for Bertie, who dutifully leaps to my side, snorts, rests his small, flat head on my chest and goes to sleep. This is where I am safest, waiting for depression to release me. This is where I still know who I am.

It was lucky, then, that Bertie was with us when my local psychiatrist couldn't prescribe my usual medication to me. We were living in London at the time, and we'd just moved to a new borough in the north-west of that grey, sprawling city. The way the National Health Service works, you have to see medical professionals in your postcode and they only have access to certain medications. I waited five months to see a local psychiatrist so that he could prescribe me the antidepressants I had been on, only for him to calmly inform me that they were not available where I lived. 'Move house or change medication,' he said, as though that were an easy choice. I opted for the latter with enormous dread, knowing from experience how ghastly it can be to change medication.

Before I could swap one smooth red pill for two new white ones, I had to taper down my dose gradually and then come off all medication for a few weeks. So that the medications didn't clash in my system, I had to exist without any chemical support for a long, aching fortnight. Hours stretched, time slowed, days passed without my being able to recognise myself. I barely knew who I was, except that I recognised this feeling from the last time I'd stopped taking medication. I couldn't work, I couldn't write, I couldn't function. Mostly, I stayed at home, between the sanctuaries of our bed and our teal velvet sofa. I sent texts to the people I cherish, informing them that I couldn't go for drinks or have coffee or string together many meaningful sentences.

I tried to explain to Jono what it feels like. I'm numb, I'd say, but it hurts. I can't access my usual stash of emotions — all I can muster right now is this dim sadness. But not even a lush sadness, a sadness that cleanses and heals, a sadness that swells from your heart and makes you feel human. This was a sadness that didn't touch me or move me. It just held onto me and suspended me from my own life.

Then I started taking the new pills, but it took more than a month for them to start making a difference. Throughout that time, my main companion was Bert. When Jono was home, he would tend to me, feed me, listen to me and make me feel loved and seen and held. He built me a tepee out of blankets and lined it with fairy lights, because that's what I'd casually described as a nice place to hide while the depression had me. Jono has this vast, bracing love for me when I'm depressed, and it is one of the many reasons I adore him as powerfully as I do. He has shown me a patience and compassion I had always craved before he came into my life. I cannot say how much I appreciate him. But he has to work, of course; he cannot stop his entire life for me when I'm bereft.

Bert, however, has no professional obligations, and so he can stay by my side around the clock. Hairy and smelly and warm, he just stuck by me all those weeks. We waited it out together, shuffling through the park, watching telly, napping to escape the day. My wonderful parents were at the end of the phone, always. My friends checked in, reminding me that I wanted to retrieve my capacity to feel joy so I could see them and hug them and laugh with them. Jono took the morning, bedtime and weekend shifts looking after me, but Bertie was there all day, every day, snout rested tenderly on my arm or my belly or my shoulder. He was conspicuously present, snoring and snuffling, chewing and sighing.

It made a profound difference to have the company of a creature who could not judge me, question me or criticise me. He had no expectations of me, except that I would give him meals, treats, walks and snuggles. His basic needs were enough to make me feel needed and accountable, but they didn't overwhelm me. I left the house to take Bert for his morning walks, when I would have simply not left the house if he hadn't been there, needed walking. Depression like that usually demands seclusion, and I could easily have become a hermit, alone in my home, unwashed and unmoving. He asked me to venture into the outside world, and that took courage, a courage that reminded me of what I could do.

*

I am not the first person to suggest that the companionship of a pet might help mitigate the symptoms of depression, or improve the life of someone who lives with a mental illness. Researchers in Portugal conducted a study in 2018 that suggests adopting a pet is beneficial for people with treatment-resistant major depressive disorder. Dr Jorge Mota-Pereira and Dr Daniela Fonte asked 33 people with acute clinical depression, all of whom had struggled to find treatment options that worked, to adopt a pet. Most took home dogs; some took home cats. As a control, they asked a further 33 depressed people without pets to take part in the study. The participants' depressive symptoms were monitored over a 12-week period. A third of the patients with pets saw their symptoms improve so drastically that they could then be reclassified as having only mild depression. In a report published in the *Journal of Psychiatric Research*, the researchers concluded that having a pet enhanced the effects of antidepressant medication.

This comes as no surprise to me at all. Once I started taking my new antidepressants, I gradually started feeling able to live my life again. I started writing, I started seeing people, I started feeling joy again. I know my medication enables me to participate in my own existence, and I know, equally, that Bertie helps me heal. I rely on my little white pills to keep me stable, but I'm jolly pleased to have Bert around, too, because he absolutely helps soothe me.

What of my suspicion, then, that dogs can smell depression on a person? Why do so many dog owners report that their faithful hound tends to know when they're in distress? How do they know to offer us comfort, in the form of snuggles, nose bumps and gentle paw-holding? Dr Stanley Coren is a renowned behavioural researcher, a professor in the Department of Psychology at the University of British Columbia in Canada, and author of many international bestsellers about dogs. He is probably one of the planet's most trusted dog behavioural experts — and so the perfect person to weigh in on my theory.

He told me that the general consensus among behavioural researchers and people who work with therapy dogs is that dogs can, in fact, tell when a human being is depressed. There is decent science which suggests that dogs will approach people they think are in distress and try to provide some kind of support, usually by seeking physical contact and cuddling. Precisely how the dogs know someone is depressed is somewhat of an open question. There are two likely explanations, Stanley says, one of which, I'm pleased to say, has something to do with the sniffing of sadness. It is thought that perhaps people secrete a particular pheromone when they're depressed, which dogs can pick up on with their superior sense of smell. They may also be able to actually smell the stress hormone, cortisol, on us. It's not something we can necessarily detect ourselves, but we've always known that dogs are better with their snouts than we are.

The second possible explanation for dogs being able to detect depression is more to do with body language and the canine capacity to understand it. When a person is depressed, they generally change the way they use their body. They tend to move around more slowly, more lethargically and perhaps more awkwardly. They adopt certain poses, like having slouched shoulders, their head down, their arms hanging by their sides as they walk, and that stance where it looks like someone's chest folds in on a hinge. Dogs are very good at reading body language, and there is some evidence that they can interpret facial expressions in human beings, so it follows that they might know when someone is melancholy, anxious or bereft.

Certainly, this is true of me when I'm depressed. I simply do not have the energy or the will to move about my life in the normal way. There's no spring in my step, no easy momentum moving me from place to place. I languish on comfortable surfaces, like sofas and beds, moving between them as slowly as possible. I generally find it extremely difficult to put one foot in front of the other; that instinct to move my body in forward motion just disappears. Of course I find it extremely plausible that Bert would notice this change in me. He's either smelled it on me or he's simply picked up that something is wrong by my general demeanour. He helps in the best way he knows how, which is by offering his cuddling services.

All of this is to imply that dogs are capable of basic empathy towards their human companions. We've done experiments on all sorts of animals — pets, primates, rodents and birds — to find out whether they have empathy. While many of those animals were found to be capable of demonstrating empathy towards their own kind, dogs seem to be exceptional in that they can show empathy towards human beings as well.

A Master's student at the University of Veterinary Medicine Vienna, Annika Huber, led a team of researchers in assessing whether dogs are capable of something called 'emotional contagion'. Emotional contagion is an important aspect of empathy, whereby the emotion being felt by another being is essentially infectious to someone who has empathy for them. It is when one person (or dog) matches their own personal emotional state to that being experienced by another person (or dog). When empathy is strong enough, you feel sad when someone else is sad, angry when they are angry, and so on. We probably think the capacity to feel like this is part of what makes us human, and certainly it is an important and rather beautiful facet of human nature — but it may also be quite natural for dogs.

So, basically, what these Viennese researchers did was set up a complex series of experiments where they put dogs in one of two rooms, played them a mix-tape of noises and judged their responses. Through a loudspeaker, they played emotional and unemotional sounds, from both dogs and humans. They played recordings of crying and laughing from humans, as well as distressed whining sounds and happy barking from a dog. They also played neutral sounds, like a human woman speaking, a blackbird singing, rain, leaves rustling in the wind and the sound of a cricket chirping.

They brought 53 dogs in with their owners, placed them on a blanket in a room and, with all sorts of clever controls so that they could verify the results were legit, they played these noises and watched for signs of emotional contagion. They analysed how each dog behaved in response to the negative, positive and neutral sounds, looking for typical signs of doggy distress, like freezing, barking, shaking, yawning or scratching. Researchers concluded, based on these dog reactions, that our canine mates are very much capable of emotional contagion.

They were more distressed by the negative sounds — crying and whining — than by any other sounds. Many of them froze for much longer, listening to the unpleasant noises, compared to when they heard the sound of a laugh or a bark. There wasn't much difference between their reactions to dog and human noises, suggesting that they're capable of empathy towards their own species as well as ours.

Another study, at the University of Tokyo, tested whether dogs yawn when someone they know or care about yawns. It is one of my favourite peculiarities of humankind: that yawning is apparently contagious between people who care about each other. Yawn contagion is known as a sign of empathy among people, so it's fascinating to find out whether dogs do it, too. The Japanese researchers observed that dogs yawned more watching a human they knew. They would also yawn in response to a person yawning, compared to when a person simply moved their mouth about randomly. The researchers here concluded that, yes, dogs do exhibit a rudimentary sort of empathy.

Since we already know they can interpret our facial expressions, respond to noises like crying and understand changes in our body language, it makes perfect sense to me that they would be able to tell what sort of emotional state a human being, especially one they know well, is in. Bertie likes to stare at me intently, as I move around our lives, and it may primarily be to suss out whether I'm going to be handling any cheese or walking past the jar we keep treats in, but it also gives him plenty of opportunity to assess my physical state. If ever I cry, whether it's audibly or silently, he will simply totter across to me, lay by my side and remain there until we have some reason to move. He is a sensitive, astute little fellow, and I'm proud that experts agree with me.

Countless articles and studies from around the world attest to the health-enhancing effects of having a pet. We know that they lower our blood pressure, reduce our production of cortisol and even help boost our immune system. We know that they make us less likely to suffer a heart attack, less prone to anxiety and better protected from loneliness. They also make us exercise more, in their simple requirement for walks. They contribute to our self-esteem, because being responsible for another living creature tends to bolster your sense of self-worth in this world. They make us more sociable, because it's almost impossible for a person to walk past a dog without saying something to their owner. I have several dog-owner friends at the local park, and we often amble along, chatting about our dogs and life in general. Dogs force us to leave the house, which is a real gift to someone with depression, whose every instinct is to stay inside.

As an introvert with depressive tendencies who also happens to work from home, I could easily go days without venturing into the outside world were it not for little Bert.

Dogs are also the most tremendous source of comfort and solace. When they tuck themselves into little balls by our side, lay their heads on our shoulders or climb onto our laps, they offer the sort of wordless affection a depressed person might need. Having Bert lie himself across my body has the most mollifying effect on me; it makes me feel grounded and grateful and alive.

And then there's the love. Having a pet is an invitation to love and be loved, without judgment, without conflict, without complication. It's a simple, innocent love. It can be the most wonderfully healing thing for a person who lives with depression. Love is not a cure, certainly not, but it's a pretty powerful remedy for someone who has most likely lost the ability to show love for herself. Depression tricks you into thinking you're worthless, but a dog will always see your worth. They will love you, even if you're absolutely no fun to be around for a while. They will love you, even when you cry or stare blankly at the television or think unkind things about yourself. And the act of loving a fluffy little being is restorative, too. It can remind you what you're capable of, and how warm it feels to care. I love Bert fiercely and consistently, even when I'm down. He is a small, stout mascot for my recovery, gently urging me to find a way to get better. My doting on him is one of the most reliable constants in my life, no matter what emotional turmoil I'm in. His presence is a gift and a tonic and I simply wouldn't do without him.

CHAPTER 2

Missy, the autism support dog

NEVER HAS A YOUNG boy spent so much time thinking about pugs. Eleven-year-old Cody Lacey loves those rotund, doughy little creatures more than just about anything else. Before he'd ever had a real-life pug waddle into his home, he'd become a connoisseur of pug paraphernalia. His bedroom is littered with pug toys, pug products and pug collectibles, although he insists he does not currently own every pug-related object available, and so must earnestly continue his quest. At night, Cody sleeps in a bed wrapped in pug-themed sheets, most likely dreaming of pugs. He knows that the first pugs were born in China, and he suspects that they were bred exclusively for the purposes of cuddling, rather than hunting or chasing or any other canine activities. He likes pugs because they're silly. He likes the noise they make, *pitter-patter*, when their dainty little feet cross the floor. He likes the way they become loaves of bread when they lie down and tuck their little paws underneath the weight of their beige barrel chests. He likes chubby pugs especially, because they're all the better to snuggle, with rolls of fat to hold onto in the embrace.

Cody lives with autism. It used to be debilitating for him: making him frightened, tense, angry. For many years growing up, he didn't like to be around people. He would get distressed easily. He would fight with his older brother, who also has autism. He would refuse to go to school. Cody has sensory processing disorder, too, which affects the way he receives information via the senses. Loud noises can be painful and troubling for him, for example. It has made the world a difficult place to exist in; somewhere he never felt entirely welcome or safe.

People with autism often get fixated on a single topic of interest and learn as much as they can about it. For Cody, that was always pugs. He made a scrapbook of pug photos to carry around at school, so he always had access to something pug-related. When he got angry or sad or scared, he'd sit down, get out his pug book and flip through the pages, gazing upon pugs, until he felt calm again. He glued pictures of pug puppies onto coloured paper, interspersed with reminders like 'Take 10 deep breaths' and 'Imagine stroking a pug'. This helped him a bit, but it wasn't always enough to dispel the moods Cody would get in. It wasn't healing enough on its own, and it wasn't enough to make Cody feel safe going about his life.

When Cody was seven, and attending a mainstream primary school, he told his parents he wanted to hurt himself, and was consequently hospitalised for suicidal ideation. His mother, Jill, became so distressed by her son's despondency that she was hospitalised herself. She is diabetic, and the stress of caring for and worrying about Cody sent her blood sugar levels dangerously high. She called the doctor, who dropped by and sent for an ambulance the moment he saw her. After a long time devoting her life almost entirely to caring for her two sons, Jill suddenly found that it was absolutely necessary to look after herself.

This was a couple of years ago now. Just after both Cody and Jill were discharged from hospital and allowed to come home, it was Cody's birthday. Neither mama nor son was really in much of a state for a party, and celebration seemed at odds with what they'd just been through. Balloons, cakes, candles, games — it would all have been utterly too much for their family. However, desperate for some sort of loveliness to mark another year of her son being alive, Jill did what she thought would make him happiest: she sourced some sweet pug content. Jill, who is quite active on social media, found the Facebook page for a roving pug café; a regular event where pug owners and pug fans are invited to come along and hang out with as many pugs as possible. She posted on the group's wall, requesting that anyone in possession of a pug send her pictures of their pets for Cody to look at.

Back when he didn't have a pug of his own, Cody liked to look at photos of pugs and use his rather powerful imagination to conjure the sense of what it might be like to stroke one. When he got angry or upset, he'd sit down cross-legged and visualise what it might be like to hug a pug. It calmed him enormously, just the thought of it. So Jill wrote about what her son had been through that year, and explained why it was so important she get some new pug pics. The response was huge. The organiser of the pug café got in touch to ask her for their home address because so many members of the Facebook page wanted to send cards and gifts. Cody was delighted and proud to receive a deluge of pug-related products from strangers. His bedroom became an even greater shrine to pugs.

The pug-related kindness didn't end there, though. When she heard what Cody and Jill had been through that year, the organiser of a pug pub event got in touch. She invited them to attend her event, which is essentially a pug party, so that Cody could meet some real living pugs. He could be their guest of honour, slobbered and shed and sat on by countless pugs for an entire day, if it would please him (which of course it would, enormously). The venue was a couple of hours' drive away, though, and Jill explained to the organiser that she just couldn't drive there and back in one day — she didn't have the stamina for it — 'But thank you so much for the thought.' The lady persisted. She would put them up overnight in a nearby hotel, if only they could get there. Jill couldn't resist such an offer and settled into the immense generosity of this stranger. She and Cody went.

When they arrived at the hotel, Cody found an enormous pug toy sitting serenely on the bed, surrounded by balloons. He named the pug Oatie, after the oat and raisin biscuits he was eating at the time, which truly is as good an inspiration for a name as any. They wrapped themselves in fluffy white dressing gowns, went swimming in the hotel pool, and made themselves at home in this loving gesture from a stranger.

The next morning, they attended the pug pub event. There was a morning session and an afternoon session —

they went to both. A full day of pug company; what could possibly be better for a pug-obsessive like Cody? The pub courtyard had been fenced off to contain an immense grumble of pugs (that is the collective noun for pugs, Cody tells me: a grumble). Cody worked the room like a movie star receiving his adoring fans. Normally shy, quiet and quick to distress in social situations, Cody was all of a sudden breezy, talkative and confident. He bent down to greet the pugs and he spoke merrily to their owners. He made jokes, he laughed. He asked questions, he smiled. Jill watched on, astonished, as her son relaxed for probably the first time ever in the company of other human beings. The change in Cody was remarkable. He was utterly transformed — a different child. Being around pugs seemed to calm him, settle him and delight him. He found the sort of joy and solace a boy should experience naturally; the sort of joy and solace that had been missing from his life until that point.

'We're going to have to get a pug,' Jill said to her husband, Darren. She didn't mention at the time that this nuggety little breed sheds their fine hair profusely, and that from that moment, the family was fated to live their lives covered head to toe in pug hair. Obviously, it's a perpetual layer of dog hair worth enduring for the happiness of their younger child.

When they got home, Jill started working on the acquisition of a pug. They were renting their home, though, and pets weren't allowed. So Jill put in a call to the estate agent to explain their situation. It's more than a pet, she explained, it's a lifeline. The estate agent rang the landlord to relay the story and Jill's request. He rang the neighbour, who ordinarily would have objected to having a pet live next door, but, once she knew what Cody had been through, readily gave her permission.

With approval to house a pug in their home, Jill immediately began the search for the perfect pug. She contacted a woman called Kristine, from a charity called Muffin Pug Rescue. Kristine's own pug is called Muffin, and whenever a new recruit arrives at her rescue centre she names them after baked goods or puddings, like Strawberry Shortcake, Chelsea Bun and Cherry Bakewell. Jill explained that she needed a very calm pug for her son.

They had a false start, with a very anxious pug, which would have been impractical for an autistic boy who was prone to his own panic. Then, a five-year-old, deaf pug came in, and Kristine knew she would be the ideal companion for Cody. This particular pug had been used for breeding and kept outside all day and night. She was weary and tender and sweet. She needed a home as much as Cody wanted to give her one.

She had lost all the teeth on the right-hand side of her mouth, so her tongue lolled out the side of her face permanently, swinging about as she moved. She was a stout, sturdy little creature, beige all over with a black face, black ears and black paws. Her eyes swivelled in their sockets, which gave her a slight air of madness. Kristine's husband drove the pug down to Jill and Cody's place — and as soon as she ambled through their front door, they knew she was the one for them.

Kristine had called this pug Doreen Soreen Cake. Cody renamed her Missy when he met her, because when she wasn't with him, he would miss her. Missy took a while to adjust to her new home, as rescue animals usually do. For a time, she simply wouldn't go for a walk. Jill would lace her into her harness and take her out onto the street, ready for a gentle wander, but Missy would refuse to move. Poor Missy thought she was being evicted, every time they went to leave the house. She was tiny, but soon this inactivity gave her a belly. Eventually, with some coaxing, Missy agreed to go for short walks, deigning to totter a bit further each day. Whenever they got in the car to go somewhere, though, she yelped and whined all the way, presumably associating car travel with a change of residence.

Nevertheless, after some time, Missy settled into her new home, humoured with love and affection and stability. She learned to trust that she belonged with this family and that they wouldn't give her up. Now, she's as confident and entitled as a pug could be. She has a set of steps that help her climb onto the sofa in the living room, where a blanket is laid out for her. She sleeps in bed with Jill and Darren because Cody's bed is too small and too difficult to get up onto. For now, Jill wakes up each morning to a sneeze from Missy directly in her face. They're planning to move house and get Cody a new bed so that Missy can sleep with him every night — something Cody says would make him very happy indeed.

Missy helps Cody live his best life. She wears a sign on her lead that indicates she's an autism support dog, and that generally lets her get into places where dogs might not ordinarily be welcome. She has been to McDonald's, Pizza Hut and Laser Quest. The Laceys plan to get her an official harness, which will make taking her everywhere with them easier.

Missy has a full wardrobe of costumes, including a rainbow tutu and a Christmas pudding outfit. She's always especially well-dressed at Christmas, when the family returns to the pug café for a festive celebration. Every December, she gets a special Christmas stocking, filled with treats and squeaky toys. Her favourite foods are chicken, melon and apple. On hot days, she gets special dog-friendly ice cream.

Missy's presence in the house is powerfully calming for Cody. Now, when he fights with his brother or gets upset, he simply finds Missy, sits down with her and soothes himself by stroking her and breathing in her doggy smell. Instead of shouting or screaming or crying, he beckons Missy to climb onto his lap and waits until his pulse slows down. When he's feeling sad, Missy gives him a reason to want to be alive. She gives him a sense of purpose, of being needed, of being loved unconditionally. Missy can't speak, so she doesn't have the capacity to judge him or say something nasty to him. In her company, Cody feels peaceful and restful and happy.

Missy feels the same about being with Cody. Her main activities include napping, eating and sitting by Cody's side. According to him, she smells of shortbread and cucumber, even though she consumes neither. She ambles cheerily about the house, snortling through the wet little nostrils on her flat face. Jill and Cody use a lot of hand signals to give her commands, like 'sit' or 'stay' or 'come', because she can't hear them. They clean her ears, take her to the groomer for a haircut, and wipe her face because her small, round eyes tend to leak a lot. If she gets separated from them on a walk at the park, she panics and runs in the wrong direction, so they keep a close eye on her.

When I arrive to visit Missy and Cody, Jill meets me at the door wearing a T-shirt that says *I'd rather be walking my pug* next to an enormous picture of said animal. It's not the only pug-themed shirt Jill owns. Missy, meanwhile, totters along to greet me, watches me walk into the house, sees that her family members seem to trust me, and promptly settles onto my lap.

Cody declares this day the best day ever, because he's allowed to eat the chocolate cakes I brought him for breakfast and his dad brings him a glass of ice-cold lemonade while we're chatting.

He gobbles and chats merrily about how much he loves Missy, his favourite little creature in the world. He shows me the pug scrapbooks he's made, which he still takes with him to school. He's at a special-needs school now, where he does a lot better, in a small class with an attentive teacher. Still, whenever he panics, gets sad or feels out of control, his teacher will gently remind him to sit down in a quiet spot, break out the pug book, take some deep breaths and think of Missy. At home, they spend the majority of their time together, snuggling. Cody's grandmother is considering rescuing a pug, just so they can bring more of them into the family. Jill is thinking about a second pug when they move house and have a more room for two to amble about and settle on their furniture. This is the most pug-friendly household I've ever been in. When I leave, I am covered head-to-toe in pug hair, and not at all unhappy about it. Missy licked my arm to signify that we could be friends, and frankly I'm honoured. It is a joy to see how much this one hapless little creature has changed lives. What a very good girl indeed.

*

Missy is a pet who learned how to be a support animal for Cody. There are programs all over the world now that recruit puppies with especially good dispositions and train them specifically to help someone who has a diagnosis on the autism spectrum. Usually they're labradors or golden retrievers — those great, big, faithful hounds who are so well suited to providing unflappable support to human beings. They're perfect for this sort of work because of their gentle, dependable nature, but also, in this case, because of their size and strength.

One of the most frightening things about having a child with an autism spectrum disorder is that they can have a tendency to bolt. Without any warning and without necessarily being able to communicate why they want to flee, children with autism often just run away from their families. They'll bolt in the opposite direction or run towards something that's piqued their interest, and they don't always take potential danger into account. A lot of parents caring for autistic children are relentlessly worried about their kid running onto the road, into traffic. It's enough to make every single excursion from the house stressful and frightening — things like the school drop-off, especially.

An autism support dog can be trained to stop a child from absconding like that. There's a special lead that attaches to a belt, which the child can wear so they are basically tied to the dog. For some of the time, that's just a lovely way to be connected with the dog, and to walk him or her safely. It's a nice way of making the child feel like they're in charge of looking after the dog, too. But it's also extremely helpful in times when a child might want to run, because a dog can be trained to simply sit down and use their full body strength to stop the child from being able to move. It's called anchoring, and they can do it in the case of a child's panic attack, too: keeping them where they are and making sure they're safe. When a family is walking along a pavement, for instance, the dog can steer the child so they stick to the path, keeping them safe from dangers like oncoming traffic. For this reason, many parents who have assistance dogs in the family say they feel significantly safer when their dog is present, particularly if the dog is secured to the child.

Academics conducted a study in the Republic of Ireland, asking the parents of autistic children what benefits they got from having an assistance dog around. They spoke to 134 parents or guardians who had a dog in the family, as well as 87 parents of children who were on the waiting list to be assigned a special support dog. Parents who live with a dog reported that they felt significantly safer from environmental dangers because of the pup's presence.

They also said that they felt as though strangers in public treated their child more responsibly and respectfully when the dog was around. Having an autism support dog, with their distinctive harness, was a visual cue to be sensitive around the child and, in fact, the whole family. One of the most devastating and consistently difficult aspects of raising a child with autism is public perception: the way people react when an autistic child has a tantrum in a public space. It can be isolating, confronting and humiliating, leaving some parents feeling like failures in front of other people. Parents reported that having the dog present meant that people were more likely to respond tactfully and appreciate that the child was having a tantrum not so much because they're badly behaved or poorly controlled, but because they have a serious neurobiological condition. It made them feel seen, as a family.

Parents also said that having a dog around made them feel more competent in their parenting skills and better at managing their child, compared to the group of people who are yet to have a dog in their lives. The study concluded that, overall, the presence of an assistance dog considerably improved the whole family's quality of life. It is a rousing endorsement for a type of program that's becoming more and more popular around the world.

Autistic spectrum disorders (ASD), including autism, Asperger's syndrome and atypical autism, are perhaps more common than you might expect. They're said to affect one in every 150 children across the planet. Autism is more prevalent in males, with four times as many diagnoses in young boys as girls. This could be because autism presents differently in girls, because more women are being diagnosed as adults, having always wondered why they felt as though they behaved differently from the people around them. Diagnosis of an ASD implies impairment in three areas of behaviour: social interaction; communication or language; and a restricted range of interests and activities. It's a complex neurobiological condition with a strong genetic basis, although there is still so much about it we do not yet understand.

An encouraging body of research strongly suggests that something as simple as the presence of a dog, either as a permanent companion or just during therapy visits, can be extremely helpful. It has been shown to help autistic children better develop motor skills, and tends to make them more willing, even able, to speak. A lot of autistic children struggle to communicate, especially because they have difficulty interpreting social cues, facial expressions and body language. Consider, then, bringing in a dog to be near that child. The language of dogs is fairly simple for us to understand, and doesn't rely on verbal cues.

A dog's actions, too, are repeatable and predictable. Whether it's a game of fetch, where the dog brings back a thrown ball over and over, or a set of commands they follow, or simply the routine of their needing to go outside for a walk, there is tremendous comfort in the routine of a dog. It's soothing to know what to expect from them and to have them expect so little from you. For a child with an autism diagnosis, imagine what an utter relief this could be, in a world that otherwise expects so much more than they so often feel they can do.

Experts say that communicating with a dog may actually help kids with autism prepare for learning the subtler cues of human beings. They might be able to graduate from understanding a dog's simple requests to being better able to interpret what people might want or expect. Things like body language and facial expressions might be less confusing for them if they've spent time trying to understand a puppy. The presence of a dog also seems to encourage non-verbal or quiet, withdrawn children to attempt speaking. Therapists who invite dogs into their sessions with children have observed that kids are more likely to speak to them when a dog is present, even if it is just to enquire about their new canine friend.

Of course, it's not the first time someone in that capacity has noticed the calming, coaxing effects of a dog. We credit Boris Levenson as the first man to bring dog therapy to America, which he did in the 1960s with his dog Jingles. Actually, though, a somewhat better-known Austrian psychoanalyst by the name Sigmund Freud was taking his chow-chow, Jofi, to sessions with children earlier on in the 20th century. He claimed that the dog was there for him, to make him feel calmer, but he also liked to think of Jofi as a character analyst who would help Freud read the emotional states of his patients. Today, therapists bring dogs into their sessions with autistic children to do precisely that, as well as encourage them to be chattier, more relaxed and more open.

Another study compared the behaviour of children hanging out with a dog to the behaviour of children who were simply given a stuffed toy. They found that the kids who got to be around real dogs were less distracted, in a more playful mood, and more aware of their social environment than their peers who were stuck holding a teddy. Children were also more likely to talk when they had the real-life pup by their side. We truly cannot overstate how important that could be for a demographic of children who cannot or do not choose to speak because of their condition.

Research also tells us that having dogs around autistic kids makes them less aggressive and less self-absorbed, which are again two very confronting difficulties of raising a child with an autism diagnosis. There were, perhaps unsurprisingly, more smiles, more eye contact and more affectionate behaviour among the kids who hung out with dogs.

This could be because of the powerful calming and comforting effect dogs have on human beings. Scientists in Canada did an experiment to test the way dogs affect our cortisol awakening response, which is the level of cortisol we have surge through our bodies when we wake up. Each of us wakes to a rise in cortisol, which is our most infamous stress hormone. However, when it's frequently secreted, cortisol can be very dangerous and make us more vulnerable to all sorts of illnesses and ailments. Cortisol is present when we have that evolutionary fight-or-flight instinct, it's there when we worry, and it's there when we panic. So, really, scientists were looking at whether being in the presence of dogs can lower the amount of cortisol we produce when we wake each morning.

To do that, in this case, they measured cortisol levels in the saliva of 42 children with autism spectrum disorders, prior to and during the introduction of a dog to their home, and then after a short period during which the dog was removed from their home. The introduction of a dog significantly diminished cortisol production. Before the dog came over, children had an average increase in cortisol upon waking of 58 per cent. When the dog was around, that number dropped all the way to 10 per cent. Then it jumped all the way back up to 48 per cent when the dogs were taken away, indicating that the dogs were responsible for a significant diminishing of the cortisol awakening response in kids with autism spectrum disorders. It's astonishingly good evidence of the physiological changes dogs can affect in people — particularly in kids who need some cortisol reduction. That might partially explain why the dogs have such a calming effect on these kids, reducing their anxiety and making them less prone to panic, confusion and anger.

It is both hopeful and edifying to hear how powerfully dogs can help kids who have been diagnosed with an autism spectrum disorder. These can be difficult conditions to treat and, of course, having a dog around will not completely free a person of their symptoms. But having these special, soothing creatures around — including treasures like Missy the lopsided pug — may just be one way of making people's lives more tolerable. I saw first-hand how terrific Cody was in Missy's presence, and I heard what a different boy Cody has become since she came into his life. It makes me very happy to think of all the other lives that might be changed, simply with the presence of a canine companion. Missy would be proud.

CHAPTER 3

Echo, the dog who helps kids to read

WANTING TO HAVE A baby is a tender sort of hope. We, especially we women, grow up assuming it'll be easy: you want one, you get to have one. It can be excruciating, then, to find out that, for whatever reason, you are unable to have a child. It can cause a deep grief. Aideen Steele had been married to her husband for six years when they started trying to get pregnant. When they were unable to conceive naturally, they signed up for several rounds of IVF. One of those times, it worked. Until it didn't. Until one day the doctors couldn't find a heartbeat belonging to the little someone growing inside. Aideen and her husband were devastated. When you lose a baby, you don't just farewell that living being; you watch as the future you imagined having as a family disappears.

While she was grieving, Aideen started talking to her mother-in-law, who one day mentioned that perhaps they could get a dog. They're meant to be therapeutic, she said, which might help with the mourning. But also it would be someone to love, someone to care for, someone to dote on. A small creature who needs sustenance and affection and love. Aideen herself was aware of animal therapy — she is a primary-school teacher who has taught her students to care for things like eggs, lest they crack, and caterpillars, until they become butterflies. Her school has worked with the local farm to teach the kids how to care for a delicate life, and the results with difficult students have been astonishing. That can be the effect of learning to care for someone else, a small living thing, outside yourself. Aideen knows how profoundly an animal can touch a life. So she liked the prospect of getting a dog.

However, her husband objected to the idea of getting one if they were only going to leave the dog at home all day without supervision and company while they were at work. So he said to Aideen that if she could find a way to have the dog looked after during working hours, he would agree to having one in their home. It was a challenge, and perhaps a challenge was precisely what Aideen needed right then. She got to solving it.

Aideen contacted Geraldine McGaughey, the CEO of Assistance Dogs Northern Ireland. Geraldine is a former social worker who organises for specially trained dogs to be placed with people who need them, whether that's at a prison or a school, or with a family who have an autistic or disabled child. She works with dog trainer Shirley Whyte, who is ex-military and a lifelong fan of discipline. They're powerfully kind women, Geraldine and Shirley. They know better than just about anyone how profoundly a dog can change a life — which is why they've dedicated their own lives to making pups available to those who need them. They are a double act of extreme loveliness, tenderness and hard work. They are veritable pioneers in the assistance-dog industry, making exciting progress for people who can benefit from having one in their lives. Geraldine and Shirley were perfectly placed to get Aideen the dog she wanted.

Aideen had applied, you see, on behalf of her school: St Gerard's, which has 280 special-needs students in attendance.

The kids who go there have a disability or condition of some sort, or have been through something traumatic, and tend to struggle with learning in a mainstream school. Aideen's idea was to get a dog who could live with her at home, but come in every weekday to work at the school, helping the children to cope with their workload as well as their personal issues.

She was invited to a training session with Geraldine and Shirley, so she could see what sorts of dogs they worked with. Once they'd listened to what she was after, they offered her a fully trained therapy dog, who came with his own special jacket and harness, which he wears when he is doing his job. But first Aideen had to win the approval of the powers-that-be at school. She had to wrangle an endorsement from the principal and vice principal, who ended up being enthusiastically in favour of the whole plan. Then she had to get the entire board of directors to agree, too, plus the people who own the building that houses the school. Once all of that was sorted, she had, of course, to convince the parents. She gave a lot of presentations on the benefits of therapy dogs, and eventually everyone was on board with hiring a canine assistant.

Aideen was very clear about her intentions here: the dog was going to be a member of staff, with a particular job to do, for which he was specially qualified. He was not to be an idle distraction for the kids, or something to disrupt their learning. Quite the opposite: he would be there to calm the kids, to help them learn and to watch on as they did their work. It was important that the kids not think of this dog as a toy or a plaything, but rather as something closer to a teacher, or a teaching assistant perhaps.

Echo, a young black labrador, is precisely that. Ordinarily, on his own time, he's a rambunctious little fellow. When I meet him, I am immediately charmed. He is a seriously energetic dog, who greets me with the usual enthusiasm of a puppy who barely knows his own strength. But when he's got his assistance-dog jacket on, he knows that it's time to work. He's transformed: sensible, rational, discreet. He takes his job extremely seriously, so the moment he's in work mode he behaves immaculately. He knows that he's been employed to soothe children, and part of his job is to be calm, docile and neutral. He's warm, he's friendly, he's adorable, of course, but he's also gentle and approachable to any child, regardless of how inexperienced they may be in interacting with animals.

Aideen just has to say the command 'work time' and he knows how to behave. At the end of the day, when it's time to revert to being just a dog, ready to go bounding about in the park outside, Aideen says 'work all done' and he knows he can relax. He's an impressively clever fellow, this dog, impeccably trained as he is.

Echo started work at the school in February 2019. Now, he has his own file, like all the other teachers, which is filled with all the necessary paperwork for him to do his important job. He's got his schedule in there, telling him which students he needs to see and when. He's got his referral forms from each child who applies to spend time with him. He has nifty information sheets about how to handle him, how to care for him and how to say his commands.

He also has his own therapy room, where the kids come to visit him. It's lovely having a special safe space for children to come and hang out with Echo. There, they can get a some respite from the rest of their lives. A classroom assistant is always there with the child and the dog, even though they usually sit back and let the interaction happen.

There are all sorts of supplies in Echo's therapy room, like books to read and supplies to do art. It's a proper, creative space, somewhere kids can escape and recuperate from what might otherwise be a deceptively stressful experience: going to school. Kids tend to bring along any work they need to do and complete it alongside Echo, who simply knows to sit by and observe. Sometimes they choose a book to read to him.

Echo sees up to seven pupils a day, each day, and spends about 20 minutes with each one. Sometimes, to earn the right to visit Echo, the kids collect paw-print stickers in class, which are given out for good behaviour. A consistent string of nice behaviour will land them the reward of spending time with the cuddliest teaching assistant on campus.

They're also taught how to treat a dog, which is invaluable information as they grow up. Aideen has even started a program where kids in Years 9 to 11 can apply to become experts in handling Echo. After Aideen's very young students go home at 2 pm, she makes time in the afternoon to show the older kids how to look after Echo. They go on walks around the grounds together, visit other classrooms and learn how to behave around Echo, so that they can, in turn, teach other students how to behave in the presence of a dog. It's a powerfully lovely set-up, giving these children not just the chance to spend time with a sweet puppy, but also the opportunity to practise being patient, affectionate, gentle and sensible around a living being who deserves tender care.

A lot of the kids at this school really struggle to have the sorts of happy, easy childhoods we believe all children should have. They've been through trauma, they've lived difficult lives, and they've known the sort of heartbreak they just shouldn't have at their age. Their life experience sometimes belies their age; they've been through a lot for people so young. Many of them resent having to come into school and behave nicely, and resist with tantrums. Most of them would definitely benefit from some sort of traditional therapy, and certainly from seeing a healthcare professional. Many of their parents arrange that kind of support for them, but waiting lists can be dangerously, prohibitively long, and access can be unjustly hard.

In the meantime, they can get a little attention, support and peace from hanging out with Echo. It's a supplementary therapy — something that's meant to exist alongside help from other sources. Sitting down beside a night-black labrador for less than half an hour is not going to cure these kids, dissolve their problems or vanish their troubles. It's peaceful, though, and it's effective. Sometimes, it has astonishingly good results — and that means something. That's worth something to these kids. And to their parents. And to their siblings. And to Aideen.

Many working at this school have known tragedy, but they also now know what a soothing, restorative effect this sweet beloved dog Echo can have on the students who go there. He is there for them, when human company just won't suffice.

In the summer of 2019, a teenage boy from St Gerard's died. He had been waiting for a heart transplant and he got it, but he didn't survive long after. He was obviously devastatingly young to lose his life. His two best friends were distraught, but being young boys they found it difficult to express their grief or really even know what to do with it. On one of their first days back at school after their mate's death, they were sitting in the principal's office, discussing how they might get through the distress. They called Aideen, to find out whether Echo was free. Both boys had asked if they might spend time with the dog, knowing, sensing perhaps, that it might be a tiny moment of joy in an otherwise bleak time for them.

Aideen took Echo to them immediately, and he helped. He settled them, for a while. He let them focus on something outside of themselves; something friendly and approachable and familiar. He didn't have questions for them, he didn't ask them to explain how they felt, he didn't want to know what they were thinking. He didn't have anything profound to say about death, or life, or grief, or love. He didn't have anything to say at all. He just *was*. He sat by them, knowing that something was wrong, and waited while they cheered a little. After spending some time with Echo, the boys felt able to go to class for the rest of the afternoon. Echo gave them what they needed that day: a simple, wordless kind of support that no adult human being could have managed or perhaps even known how to give.

Echo is a pretty good guy to have around if you're grieving. During his time at the school so far, a young girl came into class right after her mother had died. The teachers hadn't been told what happened, but she was obviously upset and withdrawn, and asked if she could possibly go and see Echo. The way she felt, no human could have comforted her. Adults of our species tend to have too many questions and not enough quiet, unassuming affection. They have expectations, no matter how well they think they're hiding them. This girl was smiling within 15 minutes of being with Echo, and she was able to get on with her day, going back to class and getting through until home time without crying. But not without a confidence shared, first.

While this girl was in with Echo, she started whispering to him. She got nice and close, stroked him on the head and said out loud: 'Echo, my mummy died.' It was the first time she'd disclosed that information to anyone at school, and she was able to then summon the courage to tell her teachers afterwards, too. Something about Echo's sweet, patient presence gave her the permission and the comfort she needed to say what it was that had so upset her. Echo's reaction was to lick her enthusiastically on the hand, which made her giggle. A lick on the hand from a well-meaning puppy can make just about anyone laugh, even when that person's bereft. That is just the puppy effect: an infectious sort of joy that you can't help feeling, even when you've never been more miserable in your life. Dogs, especially great big gentle ones like Echo, have a magical way of infiltrating a person's sadness like that. It's special.

Echo's always changing someone's day, or altering their behaviour, or making them feel better. It's his job and he's truly very good at it. Some of the kids who attend this school really struggle: to focus, to behave, to attend classes at all. They get distracted, they get distressed, they sometimes get violent. Parents have told Aideen that they simply cannot believe the difference once their kid has been to visit Echo, or started seeing him on a regular basis. If they know they're going to see their favourite four-legged ally on a particular day, their entire disposition changes. They get up in the morning without complaint, they eat their breakfast, they board the bus, they practically bound down the path towards the school gate. That is a drastic change in behaviour for some of these kids, who ordinarily protest or have trouble with even the most basic, mundane tasks of being a schoolkid.

There's one boy in particular who used to be particularly disruptive. He could be aggressive and sometimes violent in his rages. He had two teaching assistants look after him in the classroom each day, trying to keep his behaviour in check for the sake of the other students. Now, Echo will meet this boy at the school gate every morning and escort him to class, as a way of starting his day off calmly, sweetly and with purpose. It sets this boy's intention for his school hours that day: to behave as well as Echo. At the end of the day, if the boy has been well behaved enough through lessons, Echo will be there to walk him out to the bus stop. He knows all day long that his visit with Echo is entirely dependent on his own good behaviour, so he tends to take responsibility for it. He just likes the dog that much; enough to put on a show of decent behaviour all day long. His mum says he's almost unrecognisable; she can't believe the change she's seen since he started walking around with Echo. This boy now knows how to be calm and sensible. He knows to put his head down and get his work done so that he can see his mate Echo.

It's a very simple system of rewarding good behaviour, and it works. Echo now has a reputation that precedes him. Parents who've heard that St Gerard's has a successful therapy dog seek out the school for their kids specifically so they, too, can see a positive change in their young one's behaviour.

Another of Echo's greatest achievements is the improvement of reading levels at school, which is of course a skill they can take home with them and, indeed, into their grown-up lives. A lot of kids with special needs are nervous readers who wouldn't naturally or comfortably pick up a book of their own accord and read it aloud. They're what a teacher might call disengaged or unmotivated readers; they resist having to do it, they don't enjoy it and they avoid it as much as possible, even when they're capable of comprehending the words on the page.

When kids come to visit Echo, they're encouraged to pick out a storybook and bring it along with them, which they're then invited to read out loud to Echo, who dutifully listens to them. He doesn't interrupt them, he doesn't correct their grammar, and he doesn't fuss or sigh or say anything if they can't pronounce a difficult word. He simply makes himself comfortable beside them and waits while they read him a story, seeming to listen attentively, even though perhaps he doesn't fully understand all the plot twists. It gives nervous readers a confidence they can't muster around adults, whether it be their parents or their teachers. It has the most remarkable effect. Some of these kids will start reading at home, too, once they've done it with Echo. Aideen has had parents approach her at school crying because they're so happy and so relieved to have their child feeling safe and keen enough to read.

Echo tends to have the same effect on kids who are struggling with their algebra homework or a particularly gnarly spelling test. He allows them to relax into trying their best, without the pressure of expectation from an adult human waiting to see how they go. Echo helps kids concentrate, he helps them focus on their work, and he helps them work on their cognitive skills. Sometimes they learn more effectively just because they're in his presence.

*

This is not unusual, as it happens. You'll be pleased to hear that plenty of kids have learned to read more easily and more happily because they've had the attentive, waggly audience of a dog. There's an encouraging amount of evidence now that suggests having a therapy dog sit in front of a student who must read out loud is an extremely effective strategy for making them better readers (the kids, not the dogs).

Wendy Abigail Treat did her 2013 doctorate dissertation on the subject, at the University of California in Santa Cruz. She was a special-education teacher at the South Bay

Elementary School in Seaport, California, which caters for 651 students. She also has her own certified therapy dog, Kela, who helped her conduct a year-long study with some of her students. She recruited nine students from Grades Two to Five who would attend ten reading sessions, each reading for 10–15 minutes each with her and Kela. She also assembled eight more students to take part in oral reading sessions, too; only they did so over that period without the presence of a dog. They were simply in a classroom, reading aloud to their peers instead.

All of the students chosen to participate in the study reported a learning difficulty that affected their ability to read. They were nervous, usually reluctant readers who took no joy in the task of flipping open a storybook, especially if they had to read the story out loud to people around them. Many of them indicated that they were frightened, embarrassed and nervous about reading books, both on their own and in front of other people, especially other kids. You may know the feeling yourself, if the idea of public speaking makes you sweat or you'd sooner abscond from your own life, create a new identity and go on the run than do a wedding speech or a work presentation. Stage fright affects so many people, but it's particularly concerning for these kids because reading ability can be such a powerful indicator of academic competence, confidence and success.

Before and after these reading sessions, Wendy had each of the students do a series of tests designed to measure their reading skills. They were each assessed for the rate at which they could read, the accuracy with which they could get through the pages, the fluency of their language, and how much they understood from the book. They were also interviewed before and after, as were their parents, who were able to indicate whether their kids had changed their reading behaviour at home.

Wendy also wanted to know whether reading with a dog affected a child's confidence in the act of reading, their concept of how good they might be at reading, their general attitude towards the task, and their motivation to seek out books and time to read. She asked all of the students to keep detailed reading journals, documenting their feelings and reactions to each session as well as any time they spent reading in their own time. They were given little pieces of paper which had a range of faces on them, from extremely happy (smiling) to very sad (crying, frowning), and were asked to circle which one best represented their mood before each reading session and again after, to gauge whether reading with a dog can decrease a child's anxiety about reading in general. Wendy also wanted to know whether having a dog around could actually transform the very experience of reading for these children, from something they found daunting to something proactively exciting and enjoyable. She hoped, obviously, that her experiment would prove that this is perfectly possible. Delightfully, it did.

All of the students who spent their reading time with Kela demonstrated significant gains across all measures of reading skills. They became faster and smoother at reading words and sentences, more accurate and more fluent in the way they spoke, and they understood and retained more of what they read. That's compared to before spending time doing guided oral reading with a dog, and that's compared to the children who spent their time reading without a dog. In every possible gauge of their reading and comprehension skills, they improved.

Wendy described the changes as dramatic — again, measured against their younger selves and their peers who did not enjoy the privilege of dog-time. There was an increase in comprehension, for example, of 11.5 per cent in the classroom with the dog, but only 6.25 per cent in the classroom without a dog. Not only that, though. The students who read to Kela also gained more confidence, compared to when they started and compared to the kids who just read aloud to one another.

They truly felt as though they were better readers as a result of hanging out with Kela, which of course is so important because confidence in reading will motivate a child to pick up a book more often.

It's a lovely cycle, really, where confidence encourages reading, the frequency of reading increases, the skills improve, which bolsters the confidence further and convinces the kid to get reading more — and so on and so on, until they consider themselves a jolly good reader. Remember, too, that we're not talking about kids who were already open to reading. We're talking about children who were actively and prohibitively nervous about reading. They hated it, they resented it, they avoided it.

Kids described being relaxed, comfortable and happy while they were reading to Kela. They all enthusiastically circled the happiest option in their line-up of faces, except for one student, who explained that she only circled the saddest face because she was upset she had to leave the dog. In their reading journals, students wrote that reading to Kela was 'great', 'awesome', 'cool', 'exciting' and 'amazing'. Many of them spoke about feeling loved, in her presence. 'She makes me like reading better,' said one. 'I'm a better reader when I'm with her,' said another. And perhaps a more thorough explanation from one young boy: 'I like reading to Kela for three reasons. First, Kela is soft when I pet her. Next, she is funny — when I say the word "cookie" her ears go up. Last, she waves goodbye. Reading to Kela is fun!' Another student said: 'I'm not afraid to read when I read to Kela!'

Once Wendy analysed the content of the reading journals and looked out for certain words to indicate mood, she concluded that reading with Kela drastically decreased the anxiety these kids felt about reading, especially in front of other people. Where they had started out using words like 'embarrassed', 'scared' and 'nervous' to describe how they felt about reading, they eventually got to using words like 'comfortable', 'fun', 'soft' and 'furry' (which leaves us in little doubt as to who helped changed their minds about the task).

When Wendy interviewed the parents of these kids, she heard yet more about their lovely progress. According to their mothers and fathers, the kids took their new attitudes to reading home with them. They improved in their feelings about reading, their motivation to read, their confidence in their skills, the frequency with which they read and their willingness to read out loud. Two of the parents noted that their children read aloud to stuffed animals at home now, trying to replicate the experience of performing for Kela, and three said that their kids now read to their own household pets.

It's probably important to think about the fact that these kids weren't reading around Kela, or with Kela in the room. They were reading *to* Kela. We know that children between the ages of two and seven tend to believe that animals can understand human language. They speak to animals, both living and toy, and expect that they will know what is being said to them, even if they don't explicitly respond. Some research suggests that animism — this tendency to believe in the capacity for animals to listen to human speech and understand human language — is probably common in people older than seven, too. Younger kids are at that stage in their development, though, where they see the world through their own perspective, so because they can understand human speech, they believe any animal can. They simply aren't able, quite yet, to conceive of animals not understanding what they say. It's a sort of magic, that imagination.

It also means that when children read to a dog, they most likely assume that the dog is listening and can understand what is being said. A lot of Wendy's students specifically chose a book to read that featured a story about dogs, because they believed it would be what Kela would enjoy most. Others chose funny stories about animals because they thought she'd enjoy them. In their reading journals, many of the students called Kela a 'good listener' or otherwise mentioned the fact that she was listening to their story. Sometimes, it seems, this was just something they thought. Others, though, took Kela's body language and behaviour as evidence that she was an attentive listener who enjoyed their stories. One observed that Kela looked sad and put her head down when she heard the word 'raccoon'. They interpreted wags of Kela's tail, movement in her ears and her general disposition as proof that she was an active audience member who very much appreciated the performance they were putting on. It makes sense, then, that they might confess secrets or divulge important information to a dog in this setting. If they believe that a dog can understand what they are saying, but know that they won't respond with further questioning or any human-like expectations, of course a dog seems like a safe being to confide in.

This is not the only time a dog has helped children improve their reading skills. Lori Friesen, at the University of Alberta in America, wrote about a study in which 15 Grade Two students read aloud with her dog, Tango, for 20 minutes a week, over a school year. The majority of those students improved their reading skills by at least two grade levels over the span of that year. They also thanked Tango for being 'such a good listener'. There are other studies that show us how dogs can help kids improve their reading skills, as well as their general feelings about the act of reading.

We also know, crucially, that therapy dogs in the classroom can help vulnerable children learn to behave better. We have seen that when a dog is present for regular reading sessions, children with special-education needs tend to present fewer bad behaviours. They are often calmer and less anxious when the dog is present. We know that being in the company and vicinity of a dog can do all sorts of pleasant things for us physiologically. Stroking or making extended eye contact with a dog triggers a release of oxytocin, which is extremely comforting. Making physical contact with a dog, or in fact just seeing one, can lower our heart rate as well as our blood pressure. They can make human beings feel less pain, feel less agitated and be less prone to depression and anxiety. They can be a powerfully comforting presence, so it makes sense that children would respond to a dog's company by being calmer and better behaved. They're restorative and reassuring, for anyone except perhaps those who are frightened of dogs, allergic to dogs or unable to touch one for cultural reasons. They are extremely pleasing companions in life and, as we now know, make very competent teaching assistants.

Perhaps it isn't appropriate to put a dog into every school. Some parents and teachers will inevitably have objections. Complaints will be made about fur, or slobber, or hygiene standards. There will be allergies. There will be kids who are frightened. There will be people who prefer cats.

But what we are really hearing here — from Aideen, from Wendy and from countless other teachers and academics around the world — is that therapy dogs have a genuinely exciting capacity to help children. To help them read, sure, which is extremely important. But also to help them feel confident, calm, happy and safe, not only in the classroom but at home and in their futures. They don't just play with these sweet creatures; they trust them, they love them and they confide in them. Their days are better for having a dog in their lives. Their reading skills are improved, yep, but so too are their lives. It's a tremendous revelation, and a joyous one. With any hope, we will see more dogs like Echo trotting down the corridors of more schools, sitting patiently and waiting to hear a story.

CHAPTER 4

Pip, the diabetic alert dog

SOMETIMES, YOU'VE JUST GOT to do what's required in order to get the dog you want. Especially if you're not quite old enough to be making such a big decision for yourself and your family. For eight-year-old Katie Gregson, that meant getting approval from both her parents, neither of whom was initially at all enthused about getting a pup. Katie's mother was fairly easy to persuade, though; she can't help feeling maternal towards small living creatures, so Katie simply kept showing her photographs of puppies until she caved. Her dad, however, was a bit harder to crack. He'd had a dog before — a border collie — and when she died, he swore he could never go through that anguish again. So when his daughter began begging him for precisely that breed of dog, he didn't think he could do it. No, he said, again and again (a difficult word for a doting father to say).

Katie adapted and upgraded her campaign. She started getting stuffed-toy dogs and sticky-taping them to various surfaces and appliances, anywhere that would be sure to make it into her dad's amblings around their home. She taped stuffed-toy dogs to the microwave, to the TV, to the wall. Meanwhile, she kept on nagging, begging and pleading for a border collie pup to call her own. There was a show on telly at the time called *Mist*, which was about a border collie, and Katie had to have one of her own. She was determined — and she persisted until the job was done. It took two years, but eventually Katie's dad, David, gave in and agreed to get a dog. A border collie puppy, even after all of David's promises to himself to the contrary. Sometimes, the only way to truly recover from the grief of losing a dog is to find space in your heart for another. The look on your daughter's face when she finally meets her new best friend probably helps, too.

And so it was that sweet, wiry Pip came to live in the Gregson family home. Katie was ten years old when she first went to see Pip, an eight-week-old bundle of puppy who tumbled towards her, all tiny, tentative legs and wet button nose. Pip was there with her brother, who promptly ignored the Gregsons. Pip, however, tottered straight on over to Katie and her parents when they arrived, obviously choosing, as dogs so often do, the people she'd live with for the rest of her life. Katie adored her from the moment they met, and, really, they haven't spent much time apart since.

Katie's now 17 years old and Pip is something more than just a pet. Around the time she got Pip, Katie and her mum had read about the idea of diabetic alert dogs. They're dogs who are specially trained to detect when their human has either low or high blood sugar levels. They learn, over time, to alert someone when they smell a change in that person's blood glucose levels, to prevent them from having a hypoglycaemic (low blood sugar) and hyperglycaemic (high blood sugar) episode. A couple of years after she arrived, Pip got to learning.

Katie lives with type 1 diabetes. She was diagnosed with the condition at two years old, making her one of the youngest patients to ever be diagnosed with the condition at her local hospital. At the time, of course, she didn't have a way to properly communicate that she was feeling unwell or say what was the matter, so her parents despaired every time she'd wail.

Eventually, she came into the hospital in a critical condition — diabetes can be extremely dangerous, when it's left untreated. She had dangerously high blood sugar because her body was not producing insulin. Later, she'd have wildly differing highs and lows in blood sugar.

While she was a kid, her parents were in charge of administering her insulin, which they did with the jab of a needle multiple times each day. When Katie reached her teenage years, she started looking after herself. She's fiercely independent, she says, and it's been important to her for years that she is in control of her own condition. Type 1 diabetes is an auto-immune condition, so the incarnation of the illness has nothing to do with her lifestyle choices. It's because her pancreas doesn't do its job, and can occur in anyone, however fit or healthy. Living with the condition means Katie has to regularly check her blood sugar levels, maybe ten times a day, pricking her little finger and then using a small remote control to administer the correct amount of insulin into her blood stream via an insulin pump that's embedded in her skin. It's a full-time job, really, managing her condition. While she can eat what she likes, she has to be doing the maths on how much insulin she'll need to counteract her latest snack. It's tough, but so is she. For someone so young, she's resilient and determined and calm.

Katie has some help managing her condition now, though. At first, she had planned to keep Pip just as her companion. She taught the pup all the basic obedience commands, so Pip's a tremendously well-behaved dog who sits, stays, waits and comes all at the utterance of a particular word. Pip can do more than 50 tricks, too; silly show-off things like weaving between your legs or jumping over you. By the time she got Pip, Katie had watched a lot of *Britain's Got Talent*, and was inspired by the very clever dogs on telly who'd do various tricks, so she set about training her own show dog.

Soon after, though, she started to wonder whether Pip might be capable of an even more impressive feat. She'd started doing a bit of research into diabetic alert dogs. There wasn't much information around at the time, and it seemed like something that only really happened in America, where they seem to lead the way in conceiving of dogs as our assistants. She found a video on YouTube in which someone had taught their dog to smell whether the owner had high or low blood sugar levels. Katie watched the clip obsessively, taking inspiration for her own training regime.

Katie set about training Pip to tell when something was wrong with her blood sugar, all by herself. She followed the protocol from the YouTube video, which meant making samples of her saliva when she had high and low blood sugar. She put some of her saliva on cotton wool pads — one taken when she had high blood sugar, one taken when she had low blood sugar — and she placed them each in a small pot. She put those pots in the freezer. Then she'd take out the pots, show them to Pip and reward her with praise and a treat every time she showed any interest in the pot. She kept doing this every single day for six months.

Her first objective was to encourage Pip to simply be curious about these scent pots. From there, she prompted Pip to make a fuss when she smelled the pots, and rewarded her for every bark or squirm. Then she'd hold the pots up to her mouth, to indicate to Pip that the smell was associated with her. Over a period of about 18 months, Pip learned to detect that smell, associate it with Katie and alert someone when she smelled it. When she was ready, Katie got rid of the pots and knew she could rely on Pip to sniff out any change in blood sugar. When Katie was younger, the idea was to get Pip to alert Katie's parents if her blood sugar was too high or too low so they could come and help.

Katie was 13 by the time Pip knew how to sniff changes in Katie's blood sugar and alert her parents. It can be helpful sometimes during the day, but really Katie has her waking hours covered. She checks herself constantly when she's up and about during the day, so she doesn't rely on Pip so much then. It's at night-time, when Katie's asleep, that Pip really does her most important work. Pip lies curled up in her own bed in Katie's bedroom, and she basically stays half-awake all night, alert in case there's a change in Katie's smell. If she smells a shift in Katie's blood sugar, she belts out of the bedroom, scampers down the stairs, pushes open the door to Katie's parents' room and waggles from one side of the bed to the other until one of them wakes up and goes upstairs to help Katie. She doesn't bark, so much as place her body in their personal space until they take notice. She's also found out that whacking her thick tail against the wardrobe is an effective, noisy way to rouse Katie's parents. Once they're awake, they go into Katie's room, wake her and get her to adjust her insulin to prevent her from slipping into a coma or needing further help.

Pip could, presumably, be trained to wake Katie, now that Katie's old enough to deal with insulin administration herself, but Pip's entrenched habit is to seek out her parents and make the alert. She does it when they're all at home together and awake, too. If they're lounging around at home in the evening and Katie's blood sugar changes, Pip will jump onto one of them and stand with her full weight on their belly or chest or lap until they get up to help Katie.

David says that he and his wife are woken by Pip at least once a week these days, so it's an extremely helpful and important routine Pip's got going. She's basically a shift-worker now, awake during the night when everyone else is asleep, constantly on alert for changes in Katie's blood sugar. When Katie gets up in the morning, dear sweet Pip gives herself permission to sleep. She curls up and snoozes through half the day, often not getting up out of bed until noon. She can be slow and groggy throughout the day, taking the time when Katie was at school — or is now at her new job — to recover from her evening patrol.

It was difficult training Pip. There were days when Katie almost gave up, days when it seemed like a patently ridiculous idea that this could ever work. She did give up, once, for three weeks. She just decided that perhaps Pip wasn't cut out for this kind of work, that perhaps it wasn't going to be possible, after all the hours they'd spent trying to learn together. And that's exactly when it clicked for Pip and she started to understand what she had to do. All of those hours finally paid off, and she showed Katie and her family what she could do.

It was life-changing to have someone who can watch over Katie at night when she's sleeping. That's when some of her most severe and dangerous episodes happen, so it's invaluable to have a four-legged night nurse on duty each night in her bedroom. It's quite remarkable, what they've been able to achieve together, and a testament to the incredible bond they have, human and dog.

Katie had a lot of time for dog training through her school years because she was home-schooled from the age of 11. When she was growing up she had a chronic pain condition that affected her shoulder and arm as well as the type 1 diabetes, and her school told Katie's parents that they could not guarantee her safety during school hours. David had retired by then, so he and his wife took it upon themselves to teach her. She could make time during the day, in the evenings and on weekends, then, to spend with Pip, teaching her and coaxing her into being the diabetic alert dog she needed.

Now, Pip doesn't miss an opportunity to alert Katie's parents to her condition. Sometimes, though, she gets confused and alerts a stranger nearby — a waitress at a restaurant they're at, for instance. But she pretty much always gets it right — even, bizarrely, when she's not in Katie's immediate vicinity. David says that he was once with Pip 30 miles from where Katie was, when the dog started doing what she usually does to alert him to a change in Katie's blood sugar. Pip couldn't possibly know, this rational man told himself, but out of curiosity he picked up the phone to check on Katie. As it happened, her blood sugar was high at the time, but she only checked because she got David's phone call. That's happened several times now over the years, that Pip has known Katie has low or high blood sugar even when they're not in the same place. There's absolutely no scientific, sensible or rational explanation for that behaviour, obviously, and the Gregsons are as sceptical as anyone, but there's something in the way their beloved dog behaves that makes them wonder what's possible. Dogs can make you believe in all sorts of impossibilities, because they're just a bit magical like that.

Katie has spent the past few years telling theatre audiences all about her remarkable experience with Pip. Her older brother, Robert, and his partner, Charlotte, studied contemporary theatre and suggested that they could do a show about Katie and Pip, simply called *Katie and Pip*. So from the age of 13, when Pip was first trained, Katie and her faithful, scent-trained hound would perform a one-hour show. Katie would tell the audience all about her condition and how she trained Pip. Then they'd do tricks together on stage. At one point, they'd release 100 tennis balls onto the stage and let Pip go for it chasing them all.

The show was really about the special bond between Katie and Pip, and each performance was very much dictated by the energy levels of both participants at the time. Katie and Robert would never ask Pip to do something she didn't want to do: the show only went ahead if Pip wanted to play and do the tricks she'd learned to do. If she showed any reluctance to do a particular trick or task, it was abandoned immediately. They started cancelling shows whenever Pip wasn't in the mood. They performed at the Edinburgh Fringe Festival two years in a row, then decided it was time to stop. Even so, Katie and Pip have contributed to a burgeoning awareness of these types of assistance dogs.

Not a lot of people have heard of diabetic alert dogs — certainly not when Katie started out training Pip, and scarcely more now. But that could be changing as we start entertaining the idea that dogs can be extremely helpful, effective and conscientious assistants when they're trained to do something specific and practical. Having Pip to monitor Katie's blood sugar levels at night-time has been genuinely life-changing for Katie — possibly even life-saving. Katie has felt safer and calmer than she would have been otherwise for the past seven years, having Pip around. She and her family are extremely grateful and, as they should be, extremely proud. It makes me wonder, truly, how many more lives we could change if we learned to trust and train the animals who live among us. We know now that diabetic alert dogs can be extremely capable, effective medical assistants, in addition to their usual duties of snuggling, walking and eating whatever treats come their way.

*

If you think that perhaps Pip is a remarkable creature and this sort of job couldn't be done by any old dog, you are perhaps quite right. Certainly dogs have different capabilities, breed to breed, but we do have some proof that suggests many dogs could learn this sort of thing. We also know how life-altering they can be.

Academic Linda Gonder Frederick at the University of Virginia did a study with 36 diabetic alert dog owners; 23 of whom were the parents of a child with diabetes, and 13 adult diabetics themselves. The majority — 61 per cent — reported that they worried far less about the incidence of hypoglycaemia and hyperglycaemia in their lives since having a specially trained diabetic alert dog. Seventy-five per cent of these owners said their dogs improved their quality of life. Seventy-five per cent said the dogs enhanced their ability to participate in physical activity.

The thing you have to understand is that these dogs may actually be more effective, timely alerts than other traditional medical technology we rely on to tell us whether we're high or low on blood sugar. Your typical blood glucose monitor can detect an abnormality in blood glucose 15 minutes after the level is too low or two high. Dogs, on the other hand, can typically alert a person to that change 30 minutes *before* it reaches danger point.

They can also detect that change before the onset of any symptoms, which is especially important for people who are no longer aware of their own changes in behaviour. Over time, diabetic patients can become unaware of the signs of an episode of hypoglycaemia, which can be extremely dangerous. If you have a dog you can outsource that task to, and rely on to alert you a full half-hour before you're in danger, what a tremendous relief it must be.

Another academic dog person, Dana Hardin at the Indiana University School of Medicine, wanted to check on the efficacy of these diabetic alert dog programs. So she evaluated six dogs, aged between one and ten years old. On average, they'd had six months of training. First, she collected sweat samples from some diabetic patients, both during a hypo and when their blood sugar was at a normal level. She placed those samples into glass vials and popped them inside steel cans. Then she arranged them in a line randomly, according to the roll of dice. The dogs were directed to this line of steel cans, and would choose the one they believed smelled like low blood sugar in a human being by sitting down beside that sample or pushing the can across the floor. The dogs would be rewarded with a treat, which was dispensed by a remotely controlled treat dispenser, so they didn't have human beings interfering with their process.

The dogs did rather well, with an accuracy rate of identifying the right cans between 89.6 and 97.9 per cent. Researchers concluded that, yes, it is certainly possible to teach a dog to reliably identify the smell of a change in blood sugar and alert someone when they do.

Funnily enough, some dogs who have never been trained seem to know when someone is having a hypo. According to research undertaken at Bristol University in 2019, one-third of dogs — even just normal, untrained pups who happen to live with a diabetic human being — change their behaviour in some way when someone has low blood sugar levels. They can smell something that we're oblivious to, with our inferior noses. So if you're in tune with your beloved pet and wonder why they're behaving differently, barking or squirming or refusing to leave you alone, then perhaps you should check your blood glucose levels. It might inspire you to train your dog so they can be even more reliable with their alerts.

It's impressive and sweet, sure, but these pups have the capacity to save lives. People have died having a hypoglycaemic episode at night-time; they're that dangerous. People can slip into a coma or have a seizure without being able to get help in time. Imagine how much calmer you'd feel having a creature sitting nearby who can tell before you can that you need to adjust your insulin.

We've come a long way, in terms of awareness and preparedness, in the time since Katie trained Pip. Now there are organisations around the world that can help train pet dogs or even provide specially trained pups to people who live with diabetes and would like the assistance. Often, the dogs and the training are in such high demand that charities can only really help people with particularly dangerous diabetes, but hopefully their scope will grow in time, as our understanding of just how life-changing dogs can be grows, and with it our investment into them.

Dogs can help us with more than just diabetes alerting, by the way. They can actually help smell a number of different illnesses, which most of the time we cannot sniff out ourselves, certainly not using the noses nature gave us. Dogs have a far superior sense of smell, as you already know. They have more than 300 million smell receptors in their noses, where we have a measly five million. They are fantastically sensitive to all sorts of smells that we simply cannot pick up on, some of which have serious implications for human health.

Dogs can smell particular types of cancer, for example, and have had impressive success in detecting it in human beings. Basically, cancerous cells leave certain odour signatures in a person's body and therefore their secretions. Dogs are sensitive enough to detect those cancer markers in a person's blood, urine and breath. Often, even if they haven't been trained to do so, they'll persist in trying to tell a person that there's something wrong. One man, for example, went to visit the doctor because his dog would not stop licking a lesion behind his ear. Once he'd had tests, he found out that it was a malignant melanoma. There are plenty of these extraordinary anecdotes from people who insist they only got checked by their doctor because their dog wouldn't give up on trying to alert them.

Dr Claire Guest, who is co-founder of the charity Medical Detection Dogs, only found out that she had breast cancer because her dog, Daisy, kept nudging a particular area of her chest, which also felt tender and bruised. She went to the doctor because her own sweet pup could presumably smell her cancer. I'm not entirely sure how Daisy knew the precise location on Claire's body, but dogs can just be unspeakably clever. Now, of course, Claire's professional mission is to help other dogs alert their humans to various conditions they might otherwise ignore or not know about.

The cancer one is obviously a game-changer. We now know that dogs can detect ovarian, breast, prostate and lung cancer, sometimes even more reliably than our existing medical tests. In 2015, for example, Italian researchers trained two female German shepherds to sniff out the chemicals associated with prostate cancer. The dogs smelled urine samples from 900 men, 360 of whom had been diagnosed with prostate cancer and 540 of whom had not. They had a 90 per cent success rate in identifying the cancer among the samples. Currently, the other tests we have to identify prostate cancer are significantly less reliable, so this is a particularly exciting development. It looks like dogs could be the most dependable way of telling whether someone has prostate cancer, which is both pleasantly surprising and absolutely wonderful.

Dogs can tell whether a person has lung cancer simply by smelling it on their breath. Spanish researchers did a test with a three-year-old labrador–pitbull cross who proved she could tell the difference between the breath of people with lung cancer and those without. She had an extremely high accuracy rate, enough to make researchers believe that we may now have a new diagnostic method.

Dogs can also smell out ovarian cancer from blood samples. Academic Heather Junqueira presented new research at the 2019 annual meeting for the American Society for Biochemistry and Molecular Biology which confirms that dogs can indeed detect lung cancer in humans. She and her research team used clicker training to teach four beagles to distinguish between blood samples from patients with lung cancer and those with normal blood serum. One beagle, called Snuggles, was unmotivated to perform the task on account of allegedly being too lazy and comfortable where he was, but the remaining three did very well. They correctly identified the samples from lung cancer patients 96.7 per cent of the time, and the normal samples 97.5 per cent of the time. Snuggles napped, and appeared to be happy with his decision.

The timely detection of cancer is particularly valuable because, as we know, early detection gives people the best possible chance of survival. Dogs are a non-invasive, inexpensive and frankly very endearing diagnostic tool — one which researchers, doctors and patients might be pleased to employ. Dogs have smell receptors that are 10,000 times more accurate than our own, so it is little surprise that they can sniff out things which evade us.

There was one woman we know of, however, who can actually smell Parkinson's disease. A Scottish lass called Joy Milne smelled Parkinson's on her husband six years before he was diagnosed. Once she'd made her claim and been proven right by doctors, she went on to correctly identify Parkinson's by people's skin swabs in an experiment. She happens to have a particularly powerful sense of smell, and she in fact alerted researchers at Manchester University to the very idea that Parkinson's might have a unique scent. Most of us wouldn't be able to smell it ourselves, and, short of getting Joy to make a living out of diagnosing strangers in a medical facility, researchers realised that they could simply call on trained dogs to do it instead. Now, organisations like Medical Detection Dogs are working to specifically train dogs to smell Parkinson's. Hopefully these dogs may even be able to tell whether someone has the illness before they present with symptoms, which obviously gives that person a head start in getting treatment.

Dogs can also help with the detection of malaria, which remains one of humanity's deadliest illnesses. Biologist James Logan did a charming and elucidating TED talk on the subject, which included an impressive demonstration from a dog named Freya. In his speech to an audience in London, he made the point that half the world's human population is still at risk of malaria. In fact, a child under the age of two years old dies from the disease every two minutes. Some people can contract malaria and pass it on without presenting symptoms themselves, which makes it particularly nasty to try to contain.

Progress in malaria research has stalled in recent years, and we do not yet have a way to eradicate it. As James explains, malaria, like other illnesses, has a distinct smell. Apparently typhoid smells like baked brown bread, TB like stale beer, and yellow fever like raw meat. To test whether dogs can sniff out the smell of malaria, researchers collected the odour of children in Gambia by getting them to wear nylon stockings. (The feet are a particularly smelly body part, so it's a helpful collection site for these smell-based experiments.) Some of the kids had been diagnosed with malaria and some had not. The researchers brought the samples back to the UK, where they got dogs to try to detect which stockings belonged to the children with malaria.

Freya the spaniel appeared on stage during James Logan's speech to demonstrate such a test, with her trainers Mark and Sarah. They put four stocking samples into pots, three of which were from uninfected kids and one of which was from someone with malaria. Freya was invited to smell the pots and make her selection. She walked promptly along the line of samples, stopping at number three to indicate that she thought this was the one that smelled like malaria. She was absolutely correct. They did the experiment again, this time removing the sample with malaria, and Freya simply walked past all of the samples, knowing that none of them was from an infected person.

Dogs have an accuracy rate of 81 per cent in detecting malaria. By the time these stockings got to Freya, they were several years old, so we might presume that the smell of malaria on a person standing in front of her right now would be much more powerful and therefore even easier to detect. The potential here is incredible; we could be using dogs more proactively to diagnose diseases like malaria across the world.

Who knows what else dogs might be able to smell? Who knows what else we can teach them to tell us? Their sense of smell is just so much better than ours. We're talking about dogs who can sometimes be more accurate in their detection of illness than other more traditional, less furry diagnostic tests. We're talking about dogs who have saved lives and could do it again. We're talking about dogs who can be taught to tell human beings when something is wrong, smell illness from body-secretion samples, and help doctors get treatment to their patients sooner. The possibilities here for the medical industry are exciting. I can't wait to hear about more dogs helping humans with their health.

As we've seen with Katie and Pip, it's perfectly possible to train an ordinary pet dog to do an important job. Pip potentially saves Katie's life once a week. She makes her feel safer and calmer and more confident in her day-to-day life. She obviously makes Katie's parents happy, too, knowing that they'll be woken up if they're needed. Pip is also just a delight. She's sweet and enthusiastic and funny. She loves going for country walks, and for some reason she's obsessed with sleeping in the car. She's a genuine, beloved member of the Gregson family. She now has a best mate, too, a poodle called Coco. They hang out together during the day while Katie is at work, and I bet they celebrate her return home each afternoon.

Pip's sleeping routine is a bit unconventional, but she lives a happy, active, loving life with her humans. She takes her job as diabetic alert dog very seriously and she does herself very proud. So does Katie, who dreams of opening her own dog-training business one day. We know well enough by now the happiness a dog can bring to a person's life. How completely wonderful that they might also bring safety, comfort and reassurance.

CHAPTER 5

Jingles, the prison therapy dog

WHEN YOU VISIT A prison, you don't expect to cradle a days-old bunny rabbit in the palm of your hand. And yet, there I was, making cooing noises, smiling ear to ear, chatting to men who'd lost their freedom. Medium-security Magilligan Prison in Limavady, Northern Ireland, is home to a menagerie of creatures in addition to the two-legged inmates. There are 11 bunnies — some black, some speckled, some a shock of pure white. There's a cardboard box full of freshly born chicks, a paddling of talkative ducks, a donkey, some goats, a modest field of sheep and a toothy ferret. None of them know or care what the 456 men who live there did to deserve their time in prison. All they want is to be fed and kept warm. They want somewhere to amble or waddle in the sun. Their unconditional affection and total lack of judgment is quietly restorative. The men who tend to them, or build and paint their homes, are easy company. They make jokes and smile freely. If I'm not mistaken, they seem to take a cheery sort of pride, maybe even a bit of childlike joy, in looking after these animals.

Perhaps the most well-known creature in this prison is Jingles. He's a rambunctious one-year-old black labrador in training to be a therapy dog. He lives with senior officer Cassandra and her family. Since his arrival, Cassandra says she's seen hardened criminals get down on all fours and roll around with him, chuckling and whispering tiny endearments. She's seen angry, burly men yelp with happiness as Jingles leaps towards them. She's seen men yell and scream at prison staff, until Jingles walks into the room and defuses the tension. She's seen men capable of doing unspeakable things soften in the presence of this endearing, sprightly pup; a creature who trades only in thick, wet licks and enthusiastic cuddles. His uncomplicated, often raucous company is an extremely welcome distraction for men who've often not known that sort of love for a long time.

With a phone call from the mental health unit, inmates are entitled to a bit of time with Jingles. Sometimes, he attends group therapy or sits beside people when they're being interviewed. He's present at hugely stressful times, and available for a bit of a reprieve from the monotony of prison life. His wriggly exuberance is an extremely effective diversion. Being in Jingles's company will lower your blood pressure and make you feel instantly calmer — it's that sweet oxytocin working its magic. You can imagine how useful that sort of pacifying effect can be in an institution filled wall-to-wall with criminals. Deployed at just the right time, a puppy's presence can make the difference between aggression and tenderness, distress and peace.

There are just three human beings on the mental health team, working with hundreds of prisoners, in a cohort where mental health problems are rife. Jingles has quickly become an important member of staff, even though he might be smellier and more prone to knocking things over than his colleagues. He can calm and comfort people quietly, quickly and without judgment.

I visit on a cool summer day. Jingles, who has just upended his bowl of water all over the floor, scampers across the room, pink tongue out, and I only just rescue my mug of sweet, hot tea in time. He whimpers softly in protest and settles at my feet while I hear from Cassandra about the healing qualities of a dog hug.

A year ago, she tells me, she noticed that some of the prisoners were missing their dogs, and she knew that others hadn't even seen one in years. They might have met search dogs who work with police, but they weren't allowed to interact with them. Wondering what sort of good a prison therapy dog might be able to do, Cassandra contacted Geraldine McGaughey at Assistance Dogs Northern Ireland to see whether they might enlist one of her therapy pups. Geraldine introduced her to Jingles, who commenced training and took up residence in Cassandra's home. He is named Jingles because he'll come running when the hefty set of keys on Cassandra's belt loop jingle as she walks, but the prisoners have been pretty vocal about wishing he was called something slightly cooler, like Boss.

Jingles, bless him, is now available to accompany prisoners on a walk around the grounds, if they'd like him to. One of his most frequent walkers is a man called Barry. Everyone calls him 'wee Barry' because the Northern Irish simply do not consider a sentence complete without use of the word 'wee'.

He's 23 and he's been in and out of prison since he was 18, twice for arson and other times for drug-related offences. He's on the autism spectrum, so he fastidiously avoids eye contact when he's trying to listen to what you're saying. It's not rude, it's just his way of concentrating. He grew up in children's homes and started committing crimes almost as soon as he was able. Wee Barry hurts himself often. When we meet, he runs his finger along a deep gash on his wrist. His face, neck and arms are strewn with cuts and scars. On days he comes to spend time with Jingles, though, he doesn't hurt himself. He looks forward to it too much; he doesn't want to risk not being allowed to see his mate.

When I ask wee Barry why he loves Jingles, he says the dog makes him feel like a worthwhile human being. Self-worth is what he struggles with most, he says, and he ordinarily doesn't think he has any. He's anxious most of the time, not to mention extremely bored. His greatest treatment, his best source of hope, the thing that makes him feel like he has some sort of purpose in this life is to hang out with one bouncy, black-haired labrador. He feels like Jingles depends on him, which is a pleasing thought for someone who feels otherwise utterly discarded and alone. Jingles gives him a reason to stay alive, a reason to wake up some mornings, and an excuse to get dressed and leave the confines of his cell. He is a solace and a friend.

Wee Barry takes Jingles for a walk — or, perhaps more accurately, Jingles takes wee Barry for a walk (until wee Barry learns how to handle Jingles). The dog is lunging forward, pulling wee Barry along behind him. Jingles stops frequently to push his entire body through the wet grass, obviously enjoying the feeling of dew on his coat. He ploughs down corridors and around corners as we cross the grounds, and almost all of Barry's fellow inmates bellow, 'Is that Jingles?' or 'Can I walk Jingles next time?'

If we get close enough, men bend down and give Jingles a scratch behind the ears or a pat on the head. They light up, in that way people do when they're all of a sudden in the presence of a good-natured dog. Some of them are working, painting sheds or cleaning windows; others are just standing around, rolling cigarettes and gossiping. Even if it's only for a passing moment, Jingles makes them happy. Just laying eyes on this daft, beautiful dog is enough to brighten their day. His presence in such a bleak, rigidly secure institution is a passing source of joy.

Meanwhile, wee Barry has decided he feels comfortable enough to chat. He's usually deathly quiet and doesn't like to talk to many of the prison staff, but with Cassandra, because she's always got Jingles by her side, he feels safe. When he has a problem or a question, he finds a way to get to her. She says this happens a lot among people who spend time with her and Jingles. Something about her alliance with a dog makes her more approachable than she otherwise may seem, in the crisp white officer's shirt and navy trousers that mark her as an authority figure. Usually, they think of her as someone to obey, rather than confide in.

Wee Barry is almost chatty in her company, making jokes and asking when he can next take Jingles for a walk (or, as the Irish call it, a 'wee dander'). While we're out for a wee dander with Jingles, wee Barry tells us he's just found out his sister is pregnant with her first child. He's now determined to stay out of jail when his current sentence is up so that he can be a good uncle. He even talks about wanting to adopt a dog when he gets a permanent place to stay. He'd get a German shepherd, if he could, something big and burly, but affectionate. However, it'll be hard for wee Barry to get a house when he's out, on account of his arson charges. He's not sure where he'll end up, but he'd like to keep spending time with dogs, if possible. Hopefully, he'll be able to stay out this time, to live a life that belongs to him and work out who he is when he's outside this place. As protective and tentatively fond as Cassandra and her colleagues might feel towards wee Barry, really their dearest hope is that they never see him again.

Before he's out, wee Barry might help build Jingles an enclosure. Cassandra has got approval to order a stack of new wood, so that the inmates can build a safe place for Jingles to play and snooze and receive visitors throughout his day. It would mean that he'd have a designated spot, right next to the mental health unit, where people could come and see him. This is a powerful vote of confidence from the prison — in Jingles and in the efficacy of dog therapy.

When Cassandra first pitched the idea of having a prison therapy dog, there was definitely some resistance. It's easy to be cynical if you haven't seen the effect a dog can have on a troubled person. Cassandra was persistent, though, and senior enough to command attention, so here we are, with Jingles nuzzling up to men who otherwise do not get any sort of tenderness in their current lives. For their part, the inmates feel like the prison is doing something positive for them, giving them a dog, and it inspires a sort of gratitude that isn't ordinarily there. The relationship between prisoners and officers has improved since Jingles arrived, because it's a break in the dynamic that usually exists between an inmate and the person who dictates what the inmate is and isn't able to do.

Jingles tends to see good in people; people who are not often paid that courtesy. Some of the men in this prison are not straight-up evil. Criminality tends to be more complicated than that, much of the time. Many of the inmates come from extremely troubled backgrounds, having dealt with various torments like abuse, assault, poverty or mental illness. They've grown up in loveless families, been treated appallingly, become addicted to a substance, or found themselves trapped in a society that, one way or another, has forgotten or neglected them. A lot of the people here are vulnerable, and many of them have never had the support they needed to become decent people. While it doesn't make what they did to get here acceptable, excusable or forgivable, it's worth thinking about the sorts of things that make someone commit a crime.

With proper care and support, maybe some of them could change. Life, for a lot of these men, is just a vicious cycle of crime, prison and release, crime, prison and release. Cassandra often sees men return, having failed to make good on their pledge to behave when they got out. She believes that Jingles could actually help some of these men salvage a life of their own and stop reoffending.

This particular prison is considering implementing a dog-training program, in addition to the animal therapy that a dog like Jingles provides. That would mean that inmates could apply to train pups to be assistance dogs. Wee Barry has already expressed interest in such a program, and hopes that while he's in prison he may be able to nab a new skill: training pups for people who need them. For a man without many prospects, the idea that he could leave this place a bit more employable is extremely enticing. For a man desperate for some sort of redemption, the opportunity to do something good is enormously appealing.

Wee Barry likes spending time with dogs and he very much wants to try to be a functioning member of society. If he were able to leave prison a dog trainer, he would be less likely to fall back in with old friends, lapse into bad habits and possibly commit another crime. If he could hold down a job, it would substantially improve his chances at having a life both he and his prison officers could take pride in. Wee Barry's track record on this is not good: he's been in and out of prison his entire adult life. He seems to feel remorse for his crimes, and he wants to earn the right to exist outside prison grounds. If he wants to show his pregnant sister that he can be the uncle she wishes he could be — present, responsible, even loving — then he needs to find a way to stay out of prison. That is his single greatest challenge, and it's one he shares with hordes of his fellow inmates. That, plus dealing with anxiety, a compulsion to self-harm, an autism diagnosis and a history of emotional instability.

*

A lot of prisoners squander their new-found freedom by committing another crime after they're released and so end up straight back in the slammer. Recidivism, or the tendency of a convicted criminal to reoffend, is one of the most serious and urgent problems justice systems around the world face. Rates of prisoners who reoffend, often within only a few years of their previous sentence ending, are deeply troubling, especially when you consider that the original prison sentence was designed specifically to be a deterrent from further criminal activity.

In the UK, the adult reoffending rate has fluctuated between 28 and 31 per cent for the past decade and a half. In Australia, 44 per cent of prisoners will reoffend after being released. In the USA, between 50 and 70 per cent of prisoners and parolees reoffend within two to three years. It's worth saying, though, that these figures are measured and reported in different ways from country to country, which makes direct comparisons difficult. Suffice to say that an alarming percentage of convicted criminals go on to reoffend, which would suggest that the prison experience is not persuasively effective in one of its primary objectives: the prevention of further crime.

Traditionally, prisons have been designed as venues for punishment. You break the law, you have your freedom taken from you, you have a deeply unpleasant experience in captivity to discourage you from doing it again, all the while keeping broader society safer. As we have seen from the above recidivism rates, though, that philosophy — that prison should be a deterrent and a place of reform — hasn't exactly been triumphant in its execution. Sure, criminals are physically removed from society and chastised for their actions, but they're not returned to their lives better people. Nor are they prevented from hurting other people or breaking further laws. Some research even suggests that prison is responsible for an increase in overall crime, rather than the obviously more preferable decrease it sets out to achieve. It's a deeply imperfect system; one that can leave people more broken than they were when they went in.

In recent years, there's been a shift in thinking across the justice system towards a more rehabilitative philosophy. People have started advocating for programs that rehabilitate prisoners, making them more responsible members of society upon their release. The idea is that prisons should try to improve the human beings who enter them, rather than simply providing unpleasant accommodation for a finite period of time and then releasing them back into society on their own. That's why so many prisoners are now able to get an education while they're incarcerated, or learn skills that will make them more employable once they emerge into the outside world again. That's why prisoners are able to garden and cook and read. That's why they're able to spend time tending to ducklings, handling a toothy ferret or training a sprightly labrador.

The very first known animal-related program in an institution came about sort of by accident. In 1975, a patient at what was then rather brutally called Lima State Hospital for the Criminally Insane found an injured sparrow in the courtyard. Secretively, he started to care for it, recruiting other patients to help him nurse the little thing back to good health. The gang were sprung when staff noticed how much their behaviour had changed. They were working together to care for the bird, which was quite extraordinary for people who usually tended to isolate themselves or get caught up in brawls. They started behaving themselves more. They showed willingness to care. They became less withdrawn and interacted nicely with the nurses and each other, all because of this broken bird. The staff chatted it over and decided that the bird should stay, but also that they would look into the potential of animals to change people they'd hitherto assumed to be irredeemable. It was a glimpse into the way caring for a living creature can alter your mood and your disposition and your attitude.

After the bird had recuperated, the hospital commissioned a study on the benefits of animal interaction for people who'd been deemed 'criminally insane'. For one year, researchers compared two wards that were the same in every way, except that one ward was all of a sudden home to some animals and the other, unluckily, was not. At the end of the 365-day study, they observed that the men who shared their ward with animals were using half the amount of medication as the fellows who lived animal-free. What's more, there was also a substantial reduction in incidents of violence among those patients, and fewer suicide attempts. Their suspicions were pleasantly proven: having creatures as housemates is indeed beneficial, especially for people who struggle with mental health problems and happen to have a nasty habit of committing crimes.

To this day, the now sensibly renamed Oakwood Forensic Centre still houses dogs, cats, parrots, goats, deer and snakes alongside its human residents. I personally cannot imagine how being in the immediate vicinity of a creature such as a snake could possibly improve a person's grasp on sanity but, happily, for some people, apparently it does. I can certainly see how a deer or goat could improve your mood, and you know by now that I'm quite fond of dogs.

In the decades since that one guy saved a sparrow, prisons around the world have chosen to place their hope for the rehabilitation of inmates in animals. Creatures, mainly dogs, are usually placed in prison environments for one of two reasons. Either they're there for animal therapy (which ordinarily requires them to wear a brightly coloured jacket when they're working) or they're enrolled as part of a program designed to rescue, train and find homes for pups who might not otherwise get that luxury.

The latter usually means the prison has partnered with an organisation like a rescue shelter, a humane society or a charity that trains assistance dogs for people with disabilities.

In some cases, dogs who would otherwise be euthanised or can't find a home are given to the prison for a period of time, assigned to an eligible prisoner and trained, to increase their chances of being adopted by someone from the general public. Other times, dogs are brought in to be trained so that they can be rehomed with people who need an assistance dog — for instance someone with autism, a physical disability or a mental health problem. In those cases, relatively well-behaved prisoners are given a dog, who sleeps in their cell with them and becomes their protégé.

An inmate who participates in the program is responsible for the pup's food, water, grooming, safety and happiness, as well as basic obedience training. These good dogs shack up with the inmate for a certain period of time — sometimes six weeks, sometimes 18 months, depending on the program. The inmate's one professional responsibility throughout that period is to care for and train the puppy, who will leave the prison knowing up to 60 basic commands. The dogs should also be able to master an agility course, which hopefully the prison has set up somewhere on the grounds. This should make them either more adoptable for someone who wants a pet, or better qualified to assist someone vulnerable who needs canine support.

The first official prison dog-training program was created in 1981 at the Washington Correction Center for Women in the USA. Inmates there could apply to train rejected dogs who were rescued by a nearby humane society and brought to the prison. Inmates would earn college credits and learn vocational skills in the program, which was also, if we're honest, a bit of a joy to participate in. Interviews with prisoners who trained dogs while incarcerated, as well as chats with their cell mates and the prison staff, reveal that they not only enjoyed this sort of work, but actively benefited from it. Many of them said that to be in charge of something so helpful and pleasurable as training a dog significantly bolstered their sense of who they were.

Programs like this are especially popular in America now, where they operate in 36 states. They're also starting to become more prevalent elsewhere, like Australia, New Zealand, Canada, England and South Africa. Studies into the efficacy of such programs regularly suggest that spending time working with dogs makes inmates more patient — both with the dogs and with other people. It improves their self-esteem, gives them the satisfaction of giving back to society, affords them more freedom to move around the prison grounds, hones their social skills, reduces loneliness, decreases stress, gives them a sense of purpose and leaves them with tangible vocational skills that could increase their chance of landing a job when they finish their sentence.

Training a dog so they can get a home is a taste of altruism for people who've possibly not been able to do that sort of thing before. In reports on some of these programs, inmates who participate have said that previously they considered themselves to be extremely selfish people, but after spending time caring for an animal they realised what it felt like to do something good for another living being. It often inspired them to be more proactively kind to other people, too, and to think about how their actions affect others. That's the thing about kindness: it's as fulfilling to be kind as it is pleasurable to receive kindness. That's a powerful experience, especially for people who've not prioritised gentleness, or tenderness, or love for a long time, possibly ever.

Dog-time also seems to have very real medical outcomes in prisons, too, as it does elsewhere. One inmate's dangerously high blood pressure and anxiety decreased after spending prolonged time with a dog. One no longer needed medication for hypertension after two months of dog training. Two discontinued their hunger strikes after a dog was placed with them. Staff and inmates regularly report that dogs make prisons feel like calmer places to live, partly because it's difficult not to smile when you're around a dog, partly because the act of being around one will lower your blood pressure and cortisol levels. A program in Ohio has reported that inmate violence had decreased by 50 per cent over a five-year period since they brought in dogs. Another one in Washington says that the average three-year recidivism rate is 28 per cent, but it's only 5 per cent for inmates who've participated in a dog-training program.

Meanwhile, dogs who are trained in prison settings are more likely to be adopted than those who are trained at a normal facility. Dogs who otherwise wouldn't have shelter or might not survive are given a home: at first, in prison, and then permanently once they leave. Prisons, of course, have to be an appropriate place for a pup to stay while they're there. They must be temperature-controlled, with heating and cooling so the dogs can be warm and cool enough. The dogs should be comfortable and safe, with a place to snooze that's soft and easy to clean. They need to be fed and have access to clean, fresh water. They should be able to look out a window and sometimes see other dogs. They need to be able to move around freely, access a secure enclosed yard for running and playing, and be able to get outside regularly.

They're ordinarily not homed with prisoners who have a history of domestic violence, child abuse or animal cruelty. Apparently, according to prison staff, the most likely outbreak of violence in the vicinity of a dog is actually because someone has said something disparaging or threatened the dog, and the inmate who's looking after the dog has retaliated. It's rare for the dog to be in danger.

There has been one desperately tragic case in America, though: a dog was killed by the man who was caring for him. The shelter who was working with that prison has now withdrawn all of their dogs. It is, obviously, unimaginably sad. Secretly, quietly, it's something I've been wondering to myself: just how safe are dogs in the care of someone who has committed a violent crime? In this one case, a man did something unspeakably cruel. As far as I know, it's the only time something like that has happened. I'm trying not to let an isolated incident cancel out the awe I've felt, hearing about how wonderful these programs can be — for the people, but also for the dogs.

Dogs are inherently good, sweet creatures. They deserve to be doted on. They deserve to be safe. They often aren't, even with members of the public, outside prison walls. With most of the people who are eligible for prison dog programs, they will be. They get a home, when they otherwise may not. They're cherished by men and women who have nothing else in their current life they can love so immediately. Eventually and hopefully, they end up living with people who will treasure them, and often with people who very much need them.

Dogs can make very real, powerful changes to a life — to mine, to wee Barry's, to countless others. They could genuinely be one of our greatest hopes for making the justice system more effective, by giving people the will and some of the skills to help them stay out of trouble. Dogs are therapeutic and unconditionally loving. They see good in a person when the rest of us can't or won't. They can be tender and affectionate and funny, which is rare and precious in a place like jail. So long as they're protected properly and treated with care, dogs can be happy there. Sometimes, it's the only home they can get.

I think about wee Barry, and the way his whole face lit up when he saw Jingles bounding towards him. I think about the way he was gamely dragged along by that sweet beast of a puppy at the end of a lead, joy writ large on both their young faces. Wee Barry has done bad things in his life, but he's also suffered bitterly, and I tend to believe he should be given the best possible chance of redeeming himself, if he's capable of doing that. His desire to live a life more decent, more worthy and more wholesome is obvious to anyone who spends time with him. His dangerous self-loathing is mitigated somewhat by the presence of a rowdy black labrador — and that makes him, and me, dare to be hopeful for his future. That's really something. That an animal could make a person want to be a better person. That a slobbery, guileless puppy could give someone a reason to keep living. Surely, it has to be worth trying?

CHAPTER 6

Poppi, the guide dog

IT'S SO EASY TO take vision for granted. To see the world, in colour, as it happens before us is a profound privilege — one we may not even fully appreciate until we properly think about living without it. Those of us who can see, even with the aid of glasses or contact lenses, cannot really know how we would react if that ability was compromised. We cannot know how completely our lives would change, how deeply we'd feel that loss.

By the time she was 18 years old, Liz Wheeler knew that she had a hereditary, degenerative eye condition called retinitis pigmentosa. She knew that it would slowly take her vision from the outside in, until she was tunnel-blind. Liz used to have really sharp eyesight when she was young; she was one of those people who could read things easily from a great distance. By the time she was 26 years old, though, Liz was declared legally blind, with less than 10 degrees of her vision remaining. In Australia, where she lives, people are declared legally blind once they can no longer see at six metres what someone else can see at 60. A person with perfectly good eyesight should have 180 degrees of vision, but someone qualifies as legally blind once they have 20 degrees or lower. Liz reached that point well before her 30th birthday, but she just wasn't ready to acknowledge it. It would take another seven years before she would properly accept and confront the fact that she can't see as much of her world as the people around her.

When Liz lost a vast portion of her eyesight, she was so scared, she wouldn't believe it, so she continued to live her life the way she always had, without asking for any sort of help. She'd walk around Sydney, commute to her high-pressure executive job and try to function as normal. Changes in light would affect her ability to see properly and sometimes she could be walking down a busy street when her eyesight would completely disappear. She cannot see in the shade, for instance, or in bright, shifting sunlight. In those moments, she'd just freeze and wait for her sight to come back.

Her eyesight was only getting worse, though. To add to her initial diagnosis, Liz also developed cystoid macular edema, which affected her central vision as well. So her world was closing in on her from the sides, and now the last remaining spot of vision in the middle of her eyeline was disappearing, too.

This was all happening so incrementally that she simply refused to properly acknowledge it. So long as she could see something — anything, even a sliver of the world around her — she held onto the pretence that she was perfectly able to function. She'd make excuses for her failing eyesight — anything but face the truth. When she couldn't see the screen of her phone, she'd say it was because the latest software update was dodgy. When she couldn't use her computer, she'd complain that technology was designed by young people with perfect vision. When she walked in front of a moving car, she'd blame the busy streets, the drivers, the distracting noise. Any failure to see could be justified away, so long as she was determined not to identify as blind. Being blind would mean that her life had to change, that she'd depend on other people, that she'd have to ask for help. She wasn't ready to do that, and she wouldn't be for some years.

But Liz being in denial didn't alter the facts and the reality they brought with them: almost every aspect of daily living was becoming significantly more difficult as her sight disappeared. So Liz basically stopped leaving the house. She'd have panic attacks all the time. She was terrified of the world, a world she could no longer see properly. She just shut down, keeping her life as small as she could make it. She framed her blindness as some sort of moral failure as though, if she had tried harder, she could have retained her eyesight. That's not true, of course, but the loss of a sense and the encroachment of a serious medical condition can play tricks with your notion of self. She was confused and bewildered and exhausted. Making your way through a life without vision, without any sort of visual aid, means that you rely more heavily on your other senses, which is exhausting. Liz would just collapse into a stupor each weekend, sleeping away as much of her life as she could. It would continue like this until the people who cared about her intervened.

One day, when Liz was 33 years old, her dad and husband joined forces to gently but firmly demand that she get some help. Together, they called her out on her delusion. You can stop fighting now, they said. You've gone blind, please let us get you the help you need. This is what we'd call Liz's critical incident: the moment she realised that she couldn't go on living the way she had been. Something needed to change, and she needed help.

A week later, someone from the not-for-profit Guide Dogs NSW/ACT came over to Liz's house to assess the situation and see what they could do. Liz started out with a cane, learning to move it about her body, detect things with it and use it to navigate the world outside. She did that for a long time, but her confidence to move about simply never returned; she was still too scared to leave the house unaccompanied. Essentially, Liz would only go out into the world when she could rely on holding her husband's arm.

After a while, Liz's orientation and mobility instructor sat her down and told her that her cane skills were good enough, but that her confidence wasn't. Life can be better than this, she seemed to be saying. She suggested that Liz might be a prime candidate for a guide dog. I'm not blind, Liz protested, or at least not blind enough. Her instructor suggested she come along to one of the guide dog experience days, even if it's just to meet the pups. It's like test-driving a car, she said, and you can see if it might work for you. Still determined to downplay the severity of her condition but unable to resist the allure of spending a day with dogs, Liz agreed.

When Liz got out of the car, she had to walk to where the dogs were waiting to meet her. Using a cane, it took her a full 20 minutes to walk that distance, unsure and unsteady on her feet. She was basically trying to follow the path with the last of her remaining field of vision. The experience of simply moving around in the world was, as ever, distressing.

Someone helped her to where the guide dogs were waiting and she was introduced to a dog. The dog was wearing a harness, which she held onto. An instructor held onto a lead as an escort, as if Liz was a learner driver in a dual-control car. Together, they started walking back the same way they'd just come, only this time the movement forward was smooth and fast and easy. The dog knew what she was doing, and guided Liz safely down the footpath at a relatively normal walking pace. She felt safe, and they covered the same ground that had taken 20 minutes in five minutes flat. Liz was delighted by the warm, comforting presence of a dog, and the easy calm with which they walked together.

Liz put her name down on a waiting list to get a guide dog of her own. From there, the lovely people at Guide Dogs NSW came over to assess her home and her family, and her life. Once they'd determined that Liz's was an appropriate place for a dog to live, they started talking about what sort of dog would suit her lifestyle. Did she need a low-energy labrador, for instance; one who would be content snoozing the day away in an office? Would she prefer an active dog? Did the dog need to be social, could it be introverted, how confident did it need to be?

Liz put in a request for a dog who was excited to be alive. She was terrified of the outside world, so she needed a dog who wasn't. She had trouble finding a reason to get out of bed in the morning, so she wanted an early riser to wake her up and get her going. Could she please have a dog who wanted to start the day at 5.30 in the morning and drag Liz along with her, she said. Seven months later, that's precisely the dog she got.

Before Poppi came to live with Liz, she was meant to spend a year living with a puppy-raising family who knew they'd just be her temporary home, socialising her and teaching her basic obedience. After ten months, though, because she's such a good and smart girl, Poppi advanced to the next level of her training. For five months, she worked with a trainer in order to become a qualified, calm, competent guide dog.

It costs A$50,000 to train a single puppy to be a guide dog. In Poppi's case, her training was funded by a bequest from a couple called Lyn and John, who had left the amount required to train one guide dog in their will. They had died within three days of one another some years ago, from different types of cancer. Theirs was a true love story, and all they really wanted was to change one person's life with their death. That person ended up being Liz. And so, thanks to the generosity of two people she had never met, her life utterly changed.

Lyn and John named Poppi after their own much-loved pet labrador. Poppi is also a place the couple loved very much: it's a slice of Italian loveliness in Tuscany, about 40 kilometres east of Florence.

Every day, Poppi does her sponsors proud. As her way of repaying, or perhaps passing on, such enormous generosity, Liz does a lot of volunteer work with Guide Dogs NSW/ACT. She tells her story to groups of people, some of whom are losing their own sight. She helps educate elderly people, young people and everyone in between about what it can be like to lose your vision, and how spectacularly the right dog can improve a visually impaired life.

Liz first met Poppi at something she calls 'guide dog camp'. It was essentially a ten-day retreat at which guide dogs and their new owners get to know each other and learn how to live together. Liz went on her own, so she could properly bond with her new companion and learn how best they could support each other. They started out in a room on their own, with plenty of treats, where they spent two hours together, just getting to know what it felt like to be in each other's company. Then, Liz learned to use the commands she'd need to navigate her life with Poppi, and they came home together. Liz was about 36 years old by this time, so it had been a full decade since she'd been declared legally blind. At last, she was ready to accept the help she needed, and sweet, enthusiastic Poppi was only too willing to provide it.

Poppi was precisely the dog Liz had requested, too. She sleeps downstairs at night now, with Liz and her husband, Dennis, upstairs in their bed, just to give them some space. She's been trained not to bark, but when she wakes at 5.30 am she makes a sort of hollering noise with her mouth, which is Liz's alarm clock. Liz has become a morning person since getting Poppi, just like she wanted, and together they go to the gym first thing most days. The gym has put a sign that reads *Guide Dogs welcome here* on their door, and they're always pleased to welcome Liz and Poppi. After they've worked out, Liz and Poppi grab a coffee down the road, and some days go into the Australian College of Applied Psychology on Elizabeth Street in Sydney, where Liz is studying to become a counsellor. Poppi sits beside her chair in the lecture theatre, snoozing away the afternoon with an occasional grumble when she gets bored. At the end of each semester, Liz allows her fellow students to give Poppi the pats they've been saving up all semester.

You mustn't pat a guide dog when she's on duty. But even though Poppi wears a harness that says *Do not pat*, strangers still reach out in public and stroke her head, her paws, her belly. This can be awkward for Liz, who knows that a guide dog needs to concentrate. Poppi is essentially functioning as Liz's eyes, so if she's distracted with affection from a stranger it puts Liz in potential danger. It also goes against all the training she's had. Poppi is food-motivated, so she enjoys a snack when she does the right thing, rather than expecting or seeking out praise in the form of pats. She's also not meant to socialise or interact with either people or animals when she's on duty, so it's confusing for her if someone new forces that on her. Liz is constantly having to explain this to people who send their kids over for a cuddle or put their hands on her dog themselves.

Liz says she's still frightened in public sometimes, not so much because she can't see what's around her, but because she can't always depend on strangers to treat her with respect. Touching Poppi against her wishes, in a way that is dangerous for her, is a gesture of disrespect. So is pushing her onto a train, grabbing her arm, touching her shoulder or entering her personal space without warning or agreement. Often people think they're being helpful, but they do not realise how frightening it might be to have someone push you or pull you or guide you along a street when you cannot see.

Other times, people are outright rude, accusing Liz of being able to see, or not being blind enough, or being too young to be blind. Something about her sightlessness gives people the impression they can get away with abusing her or taunting her or mocking her. She feels particularly threatened, obviously, when a man touches her or Poppi without their consent. Not being able to see who's right beside her makes Liz vulnerable, and she feels that every time she leaves the house.

For her part, Poppi just gets on with her job. She takes it very seriously and she really enjoys her work. Poppi knows that when she's got her harness on, it's her job to look at the world on Liz's behalf and guide her safely from one place to the next. She has been taught to look out for potential obstacles and gently but assertively guide Liz around them. When Liz takes Poppi's harness off, she knows that she can be a regular pup. She's off-duty and she has permission to be sociable and enthusiastic. She greets people, she accepts pats, she approaches other dogs for a sniff and a chat.

When I meet Poppi, she is off-duty, so she answers the door with a full-body waggle and a generous lick. I'm allowed to pat her, scratch behind her ears and rub her belly when she presents it to me. While Liz and I talk, Poppi rests her head on my feet and her bottom beside Liz's. She relaxes into a nap, occasionally lifting her head to check on Liz. She has plenty of time to just be a dog, but she actually loves to work. Sometimes Liz will take Poppi for a lap of the block just so Poppi can show Liz which things to avoid in her path, which of course earns her a treat. They have a happy life together, Liz and Poppi.

Poppi has learned to do an astonishing number of helpful things when she's on duty. If Liz needs to get into a lift, Poppi will find it, guide her there and then rest her nose above the button so Liz can press it. If Liz needs to catch a plane, Poppi will accompany her on the flight. Poppi helped walk Liz down the aisle at her brother's wedding. She can escort Liz all the way home from the local train station, a 40-minute walk which she does with a mental map of sights and smells. According to Liz's instructor, who sometimes comes to observe them together, Poppi is always looking up at Liz, trying to read her facial expression so she can gauge what she can and cannot see. She'll slow down her walking if she thinks Liz hasn't seen a crack in the pavement ahead of them, and she knows to slow down when they're walking in the shade because that's when Liz loses all vision. What Liz sees when she loses her sight, by the way, is not black. It's more a movement of fluorescent, sparkling light. Liz says it's her brain still trying to receive signals from her retina and it's a bit like a hallucination.

Perhaps my favourite thing Poppi does is help with the grocery shopping. When she and Liz arrive at the supermarket, Liz can simply say out loud the word 'milk' and Poppi will guide her to the cold section where the milk bottles sit. She knows how to show Liz the meat section, the fruit section and the bread. She also, quite remarkably, knows how to find avocados, grapes and Pepsi Max. That's Dennis's favourite drink, so Liz tried asking Poppi one time to take her to it, and the clever dog led her directly to the cold drinks aisle and stopped right in front of the cans of Pepsi Max in the fridge.

Liz has taught Poppi some of these specific requests by accident, simply because she's quite chatty and tends to talk out loud to Poppi as they move about their lives together. She first discovered that Poppi knew more English words than she had thought, when she was waiting to meet a friend one day. 'I could really do with a coffee,' she said, out loud — to herself, to Poppi, to no one in particular. Poppi promptly took Liz to the nearest café, stopped and sat down in front of the barista. Another time, when Liz also needed caffeine, Poppi took her up to a man who happened to be drinking from a takeaway coffee cup and suggested, via a nudge with her nose, that he share it with them.

Poppi communicates a lot with her snout, as many dogs do. When she and Liz board a train, Liz asks Poppi to find her an empty seat. She does that easily — please, give her a challenge. However, on an occasion where there are no empty seats, Poppi selects someone to ask for theirs. She usually picks the most able-bodied person in their vicinity, approaches them, taps them with her nose or paw and then moves her head in the opposite direction, to indicate that she thinks they should move and leave the seat for Liz to sit in. Once, when Liz and Poppi were getting a train with Liz's husband, Poppi looked about the carriage and found the person she wished to move along with a gesture of her head. She went up to a man Dennis described as having 'resting scary face'. He wasn't exactly giving out an approachable vibe, with his thick arms crossed, frowning. But there was a mother with a pram and two elderly ladies nearby, one of whom had a walking frame. Poppi had clearly assessed the situation, dismissed them as candidates for a seat swap, and proceeded to ask this man to move. According to Dennis, the man's first reaction was to frown even more severely. He looked immediately angry when Poppi approached him and moved her head to suggest he get up, but then he seemed to recognise that she was a guide dog. He understood the request, his face melted into the smile of someone who's seen how clever a good dog can be, and he promptly stood up and made way for Liz to use his seat. Dennis was astonished — and impressed.

Liz doesn't always keep moments like this to herself. She made the decision some time ago to share some of her life with Poppi online. Not too long after they started living together, she started a Facebook page. At the time of writing this, a page called Poppi the Guide Dog has over 3,000 likes. Since making the Facebook page, Liz decided to launch an Instagram for Poppi, too (@poppitheguidedog), where she has more than 2,500 followers. She mostly posts pictures of Poppi doing something, and the captions give a sweet but also informative glimpse into their lives together. With her posts, Liz rather beautifully demonstrates what it's like to have a guide dog and what it could be like to lose your sight as a human being. She made a promise to herself when she started writing about Poppi on social media to never use it to vent. If something upsetting or annoying happens in her day — like someone patting Poppi when they're not meant to or interacting with her in a way that endangers them both — she finds a way to make it educational for people who follow her. She posts helpful things, but also outrageously adorable things. Liz promotes the work of the not-for-profit who gave her Poppi, and she takes her position as a representative of theirs very seriously. Their whole online presence is a joy and a lesson — a lesson in love and courage and support and affection and duty and work. It offers a charming insight into the hope and change a dog can give someone who thinks their life as they know it is over when they lose their sight.

*

We've been using dogs as guides for people who live with blindness and low vision for a long time. There is a mural of a blind man being led by a dog found in the ruins of Herculaneum, an ancient Roman city, which dates all the way back to the 1st century AD. There's a Chinese scroll from the year 1200 in the collection of the Metropolitan Museum of Art in New York that also depicts a blind man following a dog.

We know that formal training, something like we now know it, began for guide dogs in the 1780s, at a hospital for the blind in Paris, France. By the year 1819, a man by the name of Johann Wilhelm Klein, the founder of the Institute for the Education of the Blind, included in a book some instructions for training a dog for the specific purpose of guiding the blind.

Modern guide dog training has an especially sad origin story. When soldiers returned home from World War One, some of them had been blinded by poison gas. As a German doctor called Gerhard Stalling was treating veterans for their injuries, he noticed that they enjoyed being around his dog. He had the rather brilliant idea to train other dogs to look after them. He opened a school for guide dogs in Oldenburg, Germany, in 1916. It was such a success that he went on to open more branches across the country. He was then able to oversee the training of 600 dogs a year. A decade later, in 1926, another school opened up in Potsdam, near Berlin, where they trained 12 guide dogs a month.

Around this time, a wealthy woman in America heard about all these German dogs being trained to aid the visually impaired. Dorothy Harrison Eustis was already training dogs for other jobs over in the USA. When she heard about Gerhard Stalling's school, she was enchanted by the idea of training dogs to help blind people, and she immediately travelled to Potsdam, where she stayed for some months to observe their training methods. She was so impressed by the whole operation that she wrote an article about it (titled 'The Seeing Eye') for the American *Saturday Evening Post*, in November 1927.

An American man with impaired vision, named Morris Frank, read her article and got in touch to ask Dorothy whether she might train a dog for him. He says picking up that newspaper on that day was a decision beyond price for him, because his whole life changed once he got a dog who could see for him. Dorothy agreed and trained up a dog she called Buddy, who travelled back to America and essentially became that country's first official guide dog.

In 1928, she opened a school in Switzerland, and then the whole notion of training dogs to guide the blind spread to Italy, where another specialised school was opened. The following year Dorothy opened a school in New Jersey, as the practice began to be popular worldwide. For example, four German shepherds — Flash, Judy, Meta and Folly — were trained in the UK to live with World War One veterans by 1931.

In 1950, Dr Arnold Cook, an academic, returned to Western Australia from England with the country's first guide dog. Cook, who had lost his sight by the time he was 18, heard about guide dogs when he was studying at the London School of Economics.

Many countries have adopted the idea of training dogs to be guide dogs for blind people, and now guide dogs live and work and snack and nap with their human companions all over the world.

Training programs differ slightly country to country, but generally they follow a similar pattern. Most working guide dogs are labradors, golden retrievers or a combination of the two. Poodle crosses are sometimes trained for people who have allergies, because their coats are hypoallergenic. Occasionally you get a German shepherd trained for the job and there are a few dalmatians. Essentially, guide dog candidates need to be big enough to adequately guide a human being, but also mild-tempered and calm, and intelligent enough to successfully do the training.

Usually, pups are specially bred for the job. They spend the first eight weeks of their lives just getting to know the world, maybe trying on a puppy harness and learning to climb stairs, listen to unfamiliar noises and walk past obstacles. They get many treats at this time, which is a happy thing. They sleep a lot, they receive a lot of pats. At this time, they're also being watched for their suitability. Are they calm, even when there's a strange noise? Are they brave, even if they encounter an obstacle or there's a change in light? If they pass their evaluation, they proceed to the next stage.

At eight weeks, they begin work on their obedience and behavioural skills. Then they're given to what we call puppy-raisers, who welcome these little guys and girls into their homes for about a year. During that period, they're socialised and taken out into the world to get used to busy streets, parks, shopping centres and sometimes public transport.

At six months, they get a veterinary check, because guide dogs need to be in excellent health. It's estimated that they'll walk about 9,000 kilometres in their lifetime, so they've got to be fit and able. They also have to take as few school days as possible, so they can spend as much time with their handler as they can.

At 14 months, they're no longer puppies, but dogs. To celebrate that milestone, they spend time with a trainer, upskilling and being assessed. If they're chosen to proceed, they spend the next five months learning everything they need to know in order to effectively, reliably and safely accompany someone who lives with blindness or low vision. They get plenty of rewards and downtime to just chill out, too, and trainers really make sure these dogs have a happy life. If they pass all their tests, they graduate at a special ceremony and then are matched with someone who needs them. They work as a guide dog until their age or health means they need to retire.

About 50 per cent of the dogs who start out training to become guide dogs end up graduating to do the job. It's a rigorous selection process, but also some dogs simply communicate that they don't want the job. If the trainers think a dog would be better suited to being a therapy dog in another scenario, or even just a pet, then they are redeployed accordingly. Whatever role they end up taking in a person's life, we know that living with a dog or even casually interacting with one has seriously good health benefits. The companionship that these creatures provide can help reduce loneliness, depression, and anxiety, which is invaluable for someone who has lost his or her sight.

We've probably all seen a guide dog in public at some point in our lives. We may or may not know someone who has lost some or all of their vision. Yet perhaps, until now, we hadn't thought about just how powerfully these specially trained dogs can change a person's life. Until I met Liz and her darling Poppi, I hadn't heard first-hand just how utterly transformative getting a guide dog can be for someone who cannot see the world as clearly as they'd like. I was deeply moved by Liz's story, and of course completely charmed by Poppi. May they walk smoothly, quickly and happily to the Pepsi Max section of the supermarket together for many more years to come.

CHAPTER 7

Mya, the dog who saved a veteran's life

MARK LAWRENCE IS A burly guy. He's built, and bald, with a forehead that creases when he speaks. He's ex-military and you can see it in his face, but there's also an almighty gentleness about him. I can imagine the way he would have behaved around his old dog, a jack russell–chihuahua–yorkie cross called Rocky. The dog might've reached Mark's knee if he stood on his hind legs and stretched his paws skyward —

and Mark would have bundled him up in his arms and kept him safe.

Rocky was given to Mark as a pup. The poor little guy had a heart murmur; a whooshing sound that came with every heartbeat. He wasn't predicted to live a long life, but he outlasted expectations. He made it to 15 years, all of which were spent by Mark's side, yapping and tottering and snoozing. When Rocky died, Mark was heartbroken. The grief is unspeakable when your tiniest companion goes. And it's exacerbated by people's incomprehension, when you try to explain what a dog can mean to a person, and therefore how much their absence can ache. There aren't sufficient words, really, except to say that they're family, as precious as a human being. Dog people know, though. If you talk to a dog person about grief, they'll know its cruelties and its gravity and its size. Rocky was little, but his influence in Mark's life was not.

Mark decided he wasn't ready to get another dog. Not for a long time; possibly not ever. When you're grieving, it feels like loving another dog would somehow be a betrayal. You feel like you have to stay loyal as long as possible, and reserve that space in your heart for that one departed pup. You don't feel genuine, somehow, in your love for that animal, if you move on too quickly to another one. You doubt you'd even be capable of loving another dog, anyway — isn't there only so much love each of us can muster? You're scared, too, because you know that dogs can't live forever, so falling for another mutt is simply going to end the same way one day, with this crushing sadness at their departure.

When Rocky was gone, Mark continued to turn up to his son's football games as usual, but without his mate in tow. One day one of the other dads at the game came over and asked where Rocky was. He passed away, mate, Mark said. The man told Mark that his dog had just given birth to a litter of three, and asked if he'd like to come over and see the puppies. They were border collie–springer spaniel crosses, not yet eight weeks old. You could have one, if you want, he said. Mark said no, it's too soon. He felt altogether far too tender to even know what to do with another puppy.

This man sold fruit and vegetables from home, so Mark went over the following Sunday to stock up. He had no intention of seeing the dogs; oh no, don't even suggest it. When he knocked at the door, though, he heard his mate whisper: 'Mark's here — quick, get the dogs out.' So as he walked in, three pups came tumbling around the corner. He ambled in, stood in the hall and watched them try to walk. One of them — a tiny girl dog, scarcely bigger than a handful and barely able to stand properly — fell towards him with as much purpose as a dog that size can have. She was black, with a single stripe of white dashed down the middle of her face. She was the only one of the litter who had tufts of white hair on the ends of each foot, like she was wearing socks, and a shock of white at the tip of her tail. Her ears hung perfectly by the side of her plump puppy face, flopping about and turning inside-out as she moved.

The little pup pattered across the room on soft paws she hadn't quite worked out how to use, rolled over a few times to show off, collapsed at Mark's feet, and went to sleep the moment her head touched his shoe. She snuffled and snored. She slobbered and slept. In a few groggy moments, she taught him that, yes, it is possible to find more love for a new dog, when you meet the right one. Your heart simply expands and makes room. And that was it for Mark: as far as he was concerned, he had to have this pup in his life. He came back for her four weeks later, when she was 12 weeks old and ready to leave her mama. She'd grown a little by then and she was ready to go home. Her name would be Mya.

At first, Mark intended to keep Mya as a pet. You know, a companion, someone to love and dote on, someone to sneak extra treats to under the table, someone to take for walks and look after. Eventually, though, Mya would play a much bigger role in looking after him.

Mark lives with complex PTSD after serving in the British armed forces in the 1970s and 1980s. He was at the Liverpool docks by midnight on his 18th birthday, ready to go to Belfast and fight straight out of training. He was stationed in Northern Ireland during 'the Troubles', as the IRA fought to separate Ireland from UK rule, and he saw some things he can never forget. It was essentially policy in the army that you didn't speak about any problems or issues. If you broke your ankle, you winced, you got up and you kept fighting. Mental health issues were more complicated and even more difficult to confess to. So Mark supressed his traumatic experiences, swore not to talk about them and got on with his life. He didn't ask for help until 2013. That sort of repression takes its toll on a person, in time. Eventually, he had what he'd call a complete nervous breakdown. Psychologists would say it was like taking the lid off a pressure cooker: explosive and dangerous.

When he truly wasn't coping, a mate of his got hold of someone from a charity that works with veterans. A woman arrived at his door, prepared to listen and to help him find a way to live. She noticed the bond Mark had with Mya, and how much the dog seemed to cheer him. Together, they decided to apply to the charity Veterans with Dogs, and Mark and Mya were accepted into the charity's first-ever training program. Veterans with Dogs is run by a man called Craig MacLellan, a veteran with PTSD himself, and he knows perhaps better than anyone how powerfully supportive a dog can be (his was a chocolate labrador called Fudge).

Mya was trained to be Mark's mental health assistance dog; a job that requires her to wear a very smart blue-and-white jacket. She and Mark would turn up at a facility and learn how to help each other, until she could pass an assessment on basic obedience and appropriate temperament.

The charity uses what's called bond-based training to really consolidate the relationship between human and dog. They do not use punishment or chastising; they only believe in positive reinforcement. The key to any service animal relationship is for the beast to trust the human, so they absolutely cannot be scared or expect a telling-off. The dogs are trained to pick up on things that the human needs — physical pressure when they're scared or angry, affection when they're sad, that kind of thing — and then praised for that behaviour so they know to repeat it. The dogs will learn to measure a person's mood and respond when they need support, company or physical touch. A dog's disposition is therefore very important for this line of work, and Mya is ideal, because she's calm, loyal and unflappable.

In training, Mya learned to look out for Mark in any situation. She was rewarded each time she did something that supported Mark, which means she was given treats and praise the first time she simply rested her head on his lap while he was sitting down. Over time, she's learned to read his moods and respond appropriately when he's panicky or unsure of his surroundings.

For years before he got Mya, Mark would stay at home all the time, finding it very difficult to leave the house, to go to work or to see people. Just to get through the hours he was awake, he would drink — ending up downing two bottles of red wine and half a bottle of brandy every day, not for pleasure, but for survival. He found it was the only way he could tolerate being awake, and alive.

One evening some years ago, even alcohol could not hold the pain at bay, and he made the decision to take his own life. He took out some pills and a bottle of brandy, laid them out on the table in the living room and sat down, ready to leave this world. Mya, sensing that he was in distress, put herself between Mark and his drugs. She wouldn't let him get to the table, using herself as a shield between him and his own destruction. She sat on his lap and moved her front legs onto his shoulders so they were in a full body hug (she was by then quite a lot bigger than she was as a pup). It was enough to stop him from killing himself. She reminded him, in that moment, that he had a reason to stay alive.

It wasn't the only time she saved him from himself, either; she has stopped him from killing himself twice now, each time simply providing a barrier between him and his choice of destruction. He now knows, every day, that he has to stay alive for Mya. He knows that if he tries to harm himself, she'll intervene. She can tell when he's feeling sad, when he's feeling angry and when he's feeling so bitterly down that he could opt out of this life permanently. And she's there, all the time, every time.

In fact, Mark and Mya are barely ever apart. They go everywhere together (assistance dogs are allowed everywhere except, funnily enough, military bases), and they sleep in the same bed (except on nights when Mark's partner is there, when Mya relocates to a bed less than a metre away). Their lives are utterly entwined and I suspect neither would really know, now, how to exist without the other.

Mark doesn't drink anymore; he quit alcohol and cigarettes the day he picked Mya up from his friend's house. He hasn't touched either since — he doesn't dare. Choosing to get a dog coincided with a much bigger decision in Mark's life: the decision to let himself live. Mya's arrival was an entirely new chapter for him. It has been a break from the past, in so much as that's even possible for someone whose past visits him so often and so viscerally, without warning. He made a vow to her, and to himself, that he would give himself the best possible chance of staying alive, once she started living with him. He's stayed true to that pledge every day for years now, and he swears that he simply wouldn't be here anymore if it weren't for that border collie–springer spaniel cross.

These days, Mark has good and bad days. His biggest problem is that he barely sleeps, averaging two or three hours a night. He gets violent flashbacks, night terrors and cruelly bad dreams. So as a defence mechanism his body has learned not to let him fall asleep, in case he's caught in a terror. When he does drift off and he starts to get distressed, Mya knows to do whatever she can to wake him up. If he's making noises in his sleep, she launches herself at him and licks his face until he's awake. If he's really caught in a flashback and he's not responding to her, she will paw at his face until he comes to. Sometimes Mark will wake with long scratch marks down his face, where she's had to claw at him to rouse him. He is just grateful to have someone with him who knows how to save him.

Mark doesn't cope well in public spaces, talking to new people, or going anywhere he can't immediately see an exit. He doesn't like supermarkets, for example. Too big, too public, too full of strangers. Whenever he has to go food shopping, he takes Mya with him. If he starts to panic, she can tell and simply drags him out the nearest exit. Whenever they enter any space, they both scope out the exits immediately. If they're in a public place of any kind and Mark starts to fret, Mya pulls him along with her full body strength until he's somewhere that feels safer. If he gets angry — like he did recently, when a man accidentally kicked Mya on his way past — she simply removes him from the situation and calms him down, licking his face and resting her head on his shoulder or his knee.

In 2019, he was able to attend his step-daughter's wedding and even make a speech, all because Mya made him feel safe and confident enough to be in front of a crowd. That would have been unthinkable five years ago; to even attend the wedding, let alone stand in as father of the bride. Sometimes he doesn't even recognise his own life, it's changed so much since Mya came into it.

Every day is different for Mark now, and he can't predict what his mood will be like. It helps, of course, if he's managed to get an adequate amount of undisturbed sleep. The only thing he can really depend on being consistent is that Mya will need to go out. They get out of bed at seven-ish, when he lets her outside for a wee, and then they have breakfast before heading off for a walk down by the river.

Mya does a lot of work for Mark where she has to be alert and able to navigate his moods. She knows when she's working — she wears the jacket, she puts on her best professional face — and so Mark has made her a promise that she gets plenty of time where she just gets to be a dog. So most mornings they go for a long walk together. She throws herself into the water again and again, chasing a stick, chasing a pigeon. She gets to be free and exist as an animal, which Mark thinks is really important for her. They live a good life together, the best they can.

Being in their company is lovely. Mya is demonstrably devoted to Mark, and she rarely ventures more than about three metres from his side. As we sit and chat, she stays close, monitoring the door right behind Mark, howling melodramatically when the phone rings, greeting a black labrador courteously, and intermittently rolling over on her back to present her belly for scratches. Mark tells me she doesn't put on such a display for everyone; she can tell that Mark feels safe and that he isn't alarmed by my being there, so she's free to solicit whatever pats she'd like.

She whimpers occasionally for attention, and places her impressively bearded snout on my lap from time to time, batting her eyelids at me with as much sweetness as she can muster. 'You're alright, babe,' Mark says to her quietly over and over. 'Everything's alright.' He sneaks her several treats from a bag he keeps on him at all times. She chomps them down contentedly and nestles in at Mark's feet, alert but relaxed.

To be around Mark and Mya is to be in the presence of love, to be sure. It is also to witness an extremely effective working relationship. Their bond is obvious and immense, and I truly believe they both live better lives for having one another. Mya is safe, warm, active, fit, well fed, watered, patted, entertained and doted on. She gets all the running, swimming, snuggling and snacking she could want, in exchange for her vigilance and empathy. Mark's life is markedly improved by Mya's presence in it, to the extent that he simply wouldn't be around were it not for her. They are an extremely good advertisement for assigning assistance dogs to veterans, especially those who are dealing with chronic anguish.

*

PTSD is a particularly gnarly condition. It's complicated and cruel and unrelenting. It's dangerous. It's extremely difficult to capture, and diagnose, and treat. Great hordes of people affected by it are extremely resistant to treatment, if they ever even seek it. It's especially tenacious, it seems, in the veteran community. Perhaps it's to do with the scale and nature of the trauma these people experience, perhaps it's exacerbated by a culture that doesn't encourage the disclosure of emotional distress.

In the USA, one-third of men and women who spend time in a war zone will develop PTSD. Fewer than 40 per cent of them will try to get help. If they do see someone about it, they're likely to be prescribed medication to deal with conditions like depression and anxiety, sent to group, family, psychodynamic or one-to-one therapy, or put through a course of cognitive behavioural therapy (CBT). The Anxiety Disorders Association of America reports that up to 60 per cent of people with PTSD who go through a round of CBT still meet the criteria for PTSD 12 months after treatment. None of these treatments are fantastically successful; in many, many cases, PTSD continues to overpower the person it's got a hold on.

As mentioned before, veterans are a particularly vulnerable group, with a high risk of depression, anxiety, addiction and suicide, and with very few reliable options for serious respite. People are frightened and frustrated and desperate for something that works. That's precisely why practices like pairing a veteran with a specially trained dog have become increasingly popular options — because people are increasingly desperate for anything that will help alleviate their suffering and diminish their sense of isolation. Giving someone a competent puppy to help them with companionship, security and the manifestation of their symptoms is a relatively cost-effective, low-risk complementary treatment to all the rest we've been trying.

I'm not suggesting that dogs can cure a person of an illness as serious as PTSD, or any illness for that matter — nobody is. But we're starting to hear very real and very moving accounts from veterans who live with a dog and notice vitally important differences in their lives since that dog came to stay. Veterans who use dogs as their assistance animals report lower levels of depression and anxiety and have fewer hospitalisations. They speak about feeling safer, less lonely, less sad and less panicked, better able to socialise and more likely to leave the house. They tend to take less medication than they did before they started spending time with the dog. There also seems to be less shame attached to canine therapy or assistance dogs, compared to other types of therapy. I am an advocate for all types of therapy, from psychoanalysis to music, art and dance, but there is still a stigma preventing a lot of people from openly declaring that they get it, that they need it or that they benefit from it.

Veterans, in particular, have tremendous difficulty being open and honest about their mental health problems and what they need to do to survive them. However, they seem to have less reticence about getting help from a dog; somehow it's less controversial, less indicative of some kind of weakness. Civilians, family members and strangers in public also seem to be coming around to the idea of assistance dogs accompanying people into places dogs are not usually allowed to go. Mark, for instance, has not once been challenged on his right to take Mya into a business, a building or an event. She simply wears her jacket and gets on with the business of looking after him, uncontested.

Dogs have actually been working in the military for quite a long time. Their ascension to therapy or assistance dog was quite a natural progression. In World War One, dogs were trained to help in combat. They were taught to tell the difference between uniforms, so they could correctly identify their masters from their enemies. After battle had been raging, they'd be sent out on a mission to see if there were any wounded men from their side in a particular area, perhaps somewhere humans couldn't scout. They'd sniff about and return, to tell someone whether they'd found any wounded soldiers. If they'd found none, they'd simply lie down to indicate that there was nothing to be done. If they had found someone who needed help, they'd spring into action and lead someone to where the soldier was lying, wounded.

They also learned to help men who'd lost their eyesight, like guide dogs do in ordinary situations around the world now. Eventually, people noticed how strong the bond was between men and the dogs they worked with, so they started keeping them around for companionship, too. They started enlisting them to care for the injured, alongside nurses. That's how they thought to start using dogs for therapy, particularly with men who were dealing with trauma. By the mid-20th century, more and more assistance dogs were being trained to help veterans cope with the potentially crushing fallout from war.

The first recorded assistance dog in the military was a two-kilo Yorkshire terrier known as Smoky. He is credited as the first therapy dog to get a job at war, helping nurses care for soldiers in 1944 in New Guinea. Teeny tiny Smoky was the first to officially be recognised as a therapy dog in a war zone. By 1975, an organisation called Canine Companions for Independence in Santa Rosa, California, had pioneered the concept of what Americans now call a service dog, or just a pup that was specifically trained to perform tasks that would help a veteran who had a physical disability or a mental health issue. They started running programs that taught dogs to do practical things, like picking things up, retrieving objects, switching lights on and off, pulling wheelchairs, helping people walk, opening and closing doors, carrying things, pulling owners out of bed and alerting people when someone was approaching.

Since then, people around the world have embraced the idea of training dogs to help veterans. It's still a relatively new concept, but it's getting more popular. So, too, is research on the benefits of having an assistance dog, which of course we need to justify funding these programs to get more dogs out to more veterans. In 2005, researchers observed and spoke to 20 soldiers who had returned from serving in Afghanistan and Iraq. They all had PTSD, and half of them were given psychiatric service dogs. In a survey, 82 per cent of the veterans who had dogs for the treatment of PTSD said they had fewer or less severe symptoms since getting a dog. Forty per cent said that they needed less medication once they'd started spending time with a trained dog. It may be a small study, sure, but these are actual real lives being changed — and it's not just their lives, but the lives of their loved ones and their communities, too. It's encouraging and it's deeply moving.

Meanwhile, in 2017 in Canada, academics sought to prove how effective assistance dogs can be to veterans. They gave the veterans a series of questionnaires to complete, scoring things like sleep, life satisfaction, depressive symptoms and quality of life. The veterans had to do these quizzes several times in the six months prior to getting a dog, and then again a few times after, so researchers could gauge what sort of difference a pup can make. According to the men and women in the study, dogs helped tremendously in improving how much and how well they slept, partly because they felt safe enough to doze off, knowing that their canine guardian would wake them if there was any sign of danger. They also reported a significant decrease in PTSD symptoms — things like anxiety, intrusive thoughts, mood changes and hyperarousal. Their depressive symptoms lessened. Their overall quality of life improved, as did their ability to interact with people in a social capacity. They felt more a part of their community, better able to cope with being in public places, and more comfortable leaving the house to go about their lives. Dogs seemed to give people the courage they needed to participate in their own civilian lives. So, all in all, a seriously impressive list of benefits.

The dogs we're talking about here are capable of helping their humans in a number of special ways, just like Mya did with Mark. They can tell when their human companion is anxious: they look out for when they lower their shoulders, start to breathe shallowly, change their body language and maybe start sweating. They know the signs of a panic attack, and they know it's their job to step in and defuse it. They do that by providing physical comfort, licking, hugging and sitting on their owner until they calm down. (Things we could try, between humans, but mightn't always be entirely appropriate.) They're also specifically trained to recognise the signs of a night terror taking hold, like it does with Mark, and they know to do whatever they can to rouse their person, like Mya does with her insistent licking and scratching.

These dogs also tend to make their veterans feel generally safer and more secure in the world. They know to suss out any new environment and scout any potential dangers. Most veterans with PTSD need to know where their available exits are in any room, so their dogs are trained to identify them and be ready to escort their person out in a moment's notice.

Sometimes they stand behind the veteran, to relieve that feeling like they should always be looking over their shoulder, in case of an ambush from behind — something they've been conditioned to expect after their time in a war zone. Other times, the dog might choose to stand in front of the veteran, in order to make them feel like there's a physical barrier between them and the rest of the world.

The dogs also help people relax, by climbing on top of them, resting on their lap and allowing themselves to be stroked, all of which we know can have a powerful calming effect. The consequent release of oxytocin can help modulate pain, encourage feelings of trust and comfort, and even bolster the immune system. It can increase empathy and optimism, as well as reduce feelings of fear — things you can guess would be seriously helpful to a person who's hypervigilant to attack, wounded by their time at war, and vulnerable to a visit from their past trauma at any time.

Dogs are lovely, sweet, clever beings — most of us have always known that much. It is profoundly cheering that they can be so much more than that. We're talking about creatures who can change the lives of their human companions. We're talking about friendly beasts who can mitigate the symptoms of PTSD, temper depression, weaken anxiety, encourage sleep, promote socialisation, and gift a sense of safety to someone who yearns for nothing more desperately.

Mya has utterly changed the way Mark conducts his life — and, as we heard, actually gave him back the will to live. If she hadn't been there on both the occasions he had chosen to end his life, he simply wouldn't be around. Suicide is frighteningly prevalent — among men in general, and particularly among veterans of war. When we send a human being to battle and they come back changed, wounded and less like themselves, we have a responsibility to find a way to help them heal. What if one of the most powerful ways we can salvage their lives for them is to give them a dog? Wouldn't that be something?

CHAPTER 8

Gwen, the canine court companion

GWEN THE LABRADOR DESERVES her fancy, human-sounding name. She's elegant and quiet and dignified. When she's concentrating, or receiving praise, she tilts her sweet head slightly to the side, all the better to see you. When she's prompted, she'll present a single, slender paw and place it tenderly in your palm to shake. She'll 'sit' and 'stay' and 'come', whenever she's told. She'll roll over on her back and splay her legs, like an upended beetle, if she's asked. She's obedient and polite and impeccably well behaved, even when she can smell or see food (if you've ever known a labrador, you'll know that this is quite a feat). She even naps neatly. She has a light blonde coat, sparkling night-black eyes and a big pink tongue. Gwen is one of the more refined labradors I've met, even at the tender age of two and a half years. She's powerfully serene, even when I offer her a few slivers of her favourite food, carrot. She simply opens her mouth, laps up the orange morsels from my hand and crunches enthusiastically. If she could, I'm sure she'd thank me.

I'm told she is almost always this flawless. Gwen is dead keen on being patted, and thrives on human interaction, recognition and attention. She lives for a stroke, this girl. When you lay your hand on the top of her head, or scratch the patch just under her chin, or rub her taut pink belly, she rolls her head around ever so slightly in appreciation. She does her own doggy version of a big, wide smile. She returns the love, in her own way, panting and wagging and pawing, in a very ladylike manner.

If she were a person, Gwen would make a lovely host. She could sweep you into a room and make you feel comfortable, make you feel welcome, make you feel special. She was born and bred to be a guide dog, originally. She was one of the puppies specially bred by Guide Dogs NSW/ACT in Australia, as part of their program to keep producing generations of sublime labradors who go on to help human beings in whatever way they know best.

When she arrived in this world, specifically in Sydney, she was brought into the Guide Dogs centre to be socialised with other fresh pups and learn how to behave nicely. She rolled around with her small, doe-eyed siblings and peers, licking them, pawing them, learning how to be one of them. When she was eight weeks old, she was placed with a family who would look after her for 12 months. Up until the time she was 14 months old, she learned basic obedience and simple commands. She was taught how to be comfortable in public places, hearing big noises and in unfamiliar surroundings. She was being primed for a career as a guide dog, where she would function as the eyes of a person who lives with blindness or low vision, for as many years of her life as she could give.

It's a noble profession, being a guide dog. It's an important calling, and one which many labradors are extremely happy to answer. There is great job satisfaction in the position, if you're just the right kind of dog. There is joy and pride in keeping a person safe and taking them through the world. Guide dogs need to be calm and stoic and unflappable. They have to be committed to their work and very serious about their duties.

They know, when they're fitted with a special harness, that they're working as long as they're wearing it. They're only ever truly lively and playful and enthusiastic when they're off-duty, when they have been given permission to be informal. It's a serious career for a dog, really, and those who do it get a lot out of it. With their people, they live happy, stimulating, interesting lives, having undergone years of specialised training in order to qualify for the position.

However, as we learned in the chapter on Poppi, not every pup who sets out to be a guide dog will make it; there's roughly a 50 per cent attrition rate in their ranks when they're being trained. Half the pups who start out on the road to becoming a guide dog will fulfil that purpose and go on to serve with a person who has blindness. The other half, bless them, are redeployed. They don't fail; they simply switch careers. They go in another direction. They pursue something else. At some point during their evaluation for being a guide dog, they indicated that they were not happy, not willing or not suitable for the profession. And that's OK. Not everyone can qualify for the job they set out to do, even when they're a very, very good dog.

Some of the very best dogs are selected as breeders. They're extremely good girls, girls who demonstrate the very best labrador traits. They're given to a family, so they can be loved and cared for as much as possible, and that's where they give birth to future guide dogs. Breeding dogs are chosen because they're especially calm and sweet and diligent.

If a prospective guide dog candidate is too enthusiastic, though, or is distracted, or very keen on pats, they're usually redeployed as a therapy dog instead. Guide dogs can't be motivated by affection because they're not really meant to interact with strangers. They've got to concentrate, so they're trained to do the right thing, usually for food-based rewards. Therapy dogs, on the other paw, have to be mad keen for pats. They have to be extremely comfortable with human touch and affection and physical contact. They should probably enjoy attention, because that's just what they'll get in their line of work. Therapy dogs should be sociable and enthusiastic and friendly. They should also be placid when the circumstance requires it. Therapy dogs ordinarily end up spending time cheering up the distressed or the bereaved or the unwell. It behoves them to be patient and gentle and sweet. Which, of course, we know most labradors are. They're all adorable, but the particularly affable ones make perfect therapy dogs.

Gwen, bless her, was chosen to become a therapy dog. She has the right temperament for it — she's gentle and enthusiastic and friendly. While guide dogs have to be very driven, even in the way they take up space or move around the world, Gwen's trainers noticed that she can be quite inconsistent in her pace. Sometimes she walks slowly, sometimes she walks fast. It's not a fault, it just makes her ill-suited to being a guide dog. She's also quite easily distracted. When she walks along outside, she's likely to stop and notice a bird or listen to a sound or be on the lookout for other dogs. All of these things are completely fine for a therapy dog, or indeed for a pet, but they're not quite right for someone who has to represent someone who lives with blindness or low vision. And so, sweet thing, Gwen ended up training to be a therapy dog — another noble profession.

Once it was decided that Gwen would pursue that career, she spent two weeks with a specialised trainer. Over 14 sessions, she was assessed on things like her temperament, basic obedience training and willingness to interact with people. Trainers would take her out to crowded shopping malls, busy streets and other public places to see how she'd react. They were hoping people would want to pat her and make a fuss, so they could test if she was alright with that kind of attention. Unsurprisingly, Gwen was perfect for it. She lapped it up. The trainers would take Gwen home with them during this time, too, to test out how she'd fare with their kids and their cats and their chickens. She was heavenly on all counts, patiently and cheerily accepting any affection that was given to her.

The trainers were also hoping Gwen would be quite intuitive, and sense when someone just wanted to hang out silently. Some of the people she'd meet in her line of work might not want effusive cuddles; they might just like a gentle creature to sit by them while they think, or grieve, or cry. They might like a dog to listen to them talk. Again, it turns out Gwen was naturally qualified to do exactly that.

And so, eventually, Gwen was given a job. She now works as a canine court companion. She goes in once a week, on Tuesday mornings, to comfort and greet the victims and witnesses at Burwood Court in Sydney. When she was 18 months old, Gwen was matched with a volunteer therapy dog handler called Julie Andrade, who took her home, cared for her and kept her training going. Each week, she and lovely Julie arrive just before 9 am and do the rounds, saying hello to all the sheriffs, the prosecutors and the Victim Services representatives. They make themselves available to anyone who might need a little reassurance.

Going to court, for whatever reason, is one of the most stressful experiences a person can have. It can be distressing and frightening and tense. It's unfamiliar and uncomfortable and formal and strange. What happens in court can have life-changing consequences, and so often it requires a person to give a lot of themselves, particularly if they've been the victim/survivor of a crime. The day people turn up to court, feeling unsure and unsafe, they might, for a moment, get to hang out with Gwen if they want. Julie and Gwen are allowed in the public spaces and safe rooms at Burwood Court, where they comfort and cuddle and cajole. They spend time with people who might like some distraction from what they're going through. They rarely, if ever, know the circumstances or the reason someone is at court that day. Their whole purpose is to be non-judgmental. They are an undemanding, unthreatening presence on an otherwise fraught day, ready simply to change the tone of the experience for even a moment.

It happens all the time that Gwen makes someone's day just that little bit better, right when they need it. Julie tries to remember them all. She remembers one woman who had never been to court before. She was extremely nervous and scared — and then she saw our girl Gwen. She had a labrador at home, she said, and seeing another one made her feel instantly more comfortable. She thanked Julie profusely for being there, saying that it had made all the difference to her day, just to see them.

On another day, a staff member at Burwood Court came into work inconsolable because her cat had died the night before. She asked for some time with Gwen, and now, whenever they get in, Julie pops by to check in on her. Having a bit of animal company right when you're grieving was obviously hugely comforting. Meanwhile, Julie says, there are three police officers who cannot get enough Gwen time. Whenever they come by, Gwen rolls over onto her back, knowing to expect tummy rubs. She sometimes rests her head on a police officer's foot and sneaks in a nap while they're talking business.

Julie has watched proudly as Gwen comforts children, women, men, young people, elderly people, staff, police officers, witnesses and victims. She's particularly popular with children, who can be especially frightened in court if they understand what's going on or pick up on their parent's nervous energy. When Julie takes Gwen into the safe room where victims of domestic abuse wait between sessions, they often meet mothers with babies and kids.

She remembers a time Gwen just silenced a crying toddler by gently placing her snout on his nose, which made him giggle. She remembers a child who was wailing because his teeth were coming through and his mum was discussing a complicated matter of legal protection. She and Gwen walked into the room and the whole mood changed. The tension dissipated, and the child got up, walked over and patted Gwen. When he sat down again, Gwen offered her silent support by gently resting her head on his chubby little legs. They stayed there a while, at the request of the family, just providing some light, loving relief in a tense situation.

There are countless moments like this for Gwen, who has this very special ability to brighten any room she walks into, presenting herself for snuggles, giving out enthusiastic licks or simply sitting beside someone who craves a little silent, judgment-free moral support. She is very good at what she does.

I meet Julie and Gwen on a sunny spring day in western Sydney. We sit in a park near where they live with Julie's husband and two children, aged eight and ten. When she starts trying to describe the effect Gwen can have on people, and indeed the effect she has had on her own family, Julie can't stop herself from crying. Tears stream down her face, one by one, and I get that stinging feeling in the corners of my eyes, watching her. She cries, I cry, we both cry because this dog is so sweet and so effective in her simple but profound job.

I'm so moved by Julie's generosity of spirit, her willingness to spend time doing good, and her determination to give something back to society. She came across a job ad online some time ago, advertising for the position of volunteer therapy dog handler. She knew it would mean having a dog live in her home, with her kids and her somewhat reluctant husband. He has well and truly been won over — if ever Gwen goes on the couch, which is technically against the rules for her, it's because she is comforting Julie's husband when he's had a rough day at the office.

The kids are obsessed with her, because she's magnificent and most kids dream of having a puppy in their lives. They help their mum with Gwen's ongoing training sometimes, and Gwen goes along to all of their tennis matches and football games. She is their family mascot, as well as a professional comforter of strangers. Julie says Gwen is her 'fur baby' and a genuine member of their family. She is treated accordingly, with extreme love and tenderness. She lives a good life, with one day at work a week, plus plenty of stimulating training, lots of walks in the park and time spent with both dog and human friends.

*

Gwen and Julie work as part of the Canine Court Companion program, which is run by Victim Services in the Department of Communities and Justice, within the New South Wales Government. It's a project run with Guide Dogs NSW/ACT, across ten courts in regional and central Sydney. Gwen works in Burwood, but her buddies visit places like Manly, Orange, Nowra and Wagga Wagga.

The response to the program so far has been hugely encouraging: one survey received 100 per cent positive feedback, and another had 96 per cent (we can only surmise the four per cent dissenting accounts for someone who is allergic to dogs). Of course there are always going to be some people who don't wish to interact with a dog on their day in court. Some people are too busy. Some have religious reasons they don't want to be near a dog. Some might think of themselves as cat people. That's absolutely fine; handlers like Julie never approach someone without asking if they'd like to spend some time with a dog. We need court to feel like a safe space, and the volunteers who work on this program respect that people's preferences for safety and style of comfort-seeking might differ.

Dogs make a lot of people feel comforted and happy and calm, though — enough to make it worth promoting programs like these. Stroking or making eye contact with a dog can lower our heart rate, heighten mental clarity and improve our memory function — all things that could be very useful on a day you have to appear in court. Dogs can also reduce anxiety, which is terrifically important in a stressful situation like testifying in a court case or delivering a victim impact statement. They're also an extremely pleasant distraction, capable of changing the tone of someone's experience, even if it's only for a moment. Let's face it, it's quite difficult to meet a dog like Gwen and resist smiling. Being in her presence makes you feel a bit better about the world. What a gift that could be for someone who must relive an awful experience in order to testify at court.

Hopefully, therapy dogs will become more readily available and welcome in courthouses around the world. They've been fairly popular in America, where there tends to be a more obvious, established culture of putting dogs to work and allowing them in public spaces. The first official court therapy dog recruit there was a golden labrador by the name of Jeeter. He came into court to accompany twin sisters who had to testify against their father in a sexual assault case.

The girls had, until that point, been unwilling and unable to find a way to speak up about what had happened to them. No child should have to go through that, but, given what they had been through, these girls deserved any comfort they could get. When Jeeter walked into the courtroom, they somehow found the extraordinary courage to explain what their father had done, by pointing to various parts of the dog's body.

Both girls were interviewed many years later, as teenagers, and the first thing they recalled about their day in court was that Jeeter drank water from the bathroom sink and they thought that was 'awesome'. They also distinctly remember the dog slobbering all over them. For that to be the first and most vivid memory they have of testifying in such a harrowing case is really something. It has distracted them, years later, from thinking about the very real and frightening reason they went to court that day. Their mother said Jeeter gave her daughters the chance to get over an ugly experience, and that every other victim in the world deserves to have the same opportunity.

Jeeter's first appearance in court was back in 2003. In 2004, a specially trained labrador–retriever cross started work in a prosecutor's office in Seattle. Over the decade that followed, more dogs were specifically trained to work in courthouses, many of them being permitted to go inside the actual courtroom with people who would benefit from their presence. In 2013, a very good dog named Rosie was placed in a children's home in Poughkeepsie to support a young child who had to testify against her own father in a traumatic case.

By 2018, the whole concept of having a dog in court had arrived in Europe. A labrador–retriever cross called Oliver got a job at Canterbury Christ Church University in the UK, making him potentially the first court therapy pup in Britain. Oliver's handlers say that he can sense when someone is upset and knows to stay close, whether he rests his head on their lap, falls asleep by their feet or gives them a supportive lick on the hand. He has been trained, as his peers have, not to be alarmed by any demonstration of human emotion. No matter how distressed a person gets, he knows to simply stay put and stand by them. It's that kind of quiet, unconditional support that can change a person's entire outlook on a horrendous day.

The first dog to be allowed in the courtroom in Australia was a black labrador called Coop, who started supporting victims of domestic abuse and sexual assault in 2016, in Victoria. Coop's owner and trainer, Tessa Stow, had to give evidence in a disturbing case back in 1988, so she knew how harrowing it can be, and how lonely, on that stand. Not long after that, she became a veterinary nurse and started seeing first-hand how powerful the bond between humans and their animals can be. So, she decided to train her dog so that she would be able to help people who, like Tessa, have to speak in court. It's a lovely example of one person trying to soften and rectify a pain they went through themselves, so that total strangers can perhaps feel a little less scared when they have to do the same.

Coop has since landed a job at the Office of Public Prosecutions, where she has helped more than 140 victims in more than 100 cases since she started. Most of the people she has worked with are survivors of sexual assault. There are calls elsewhere in Australia, and indeed around the world, to have dogs like Coop protect survivors of sexual assault, because they've been found to be especially effective. One woman, who doesn't want to disclose exactly what happened to her for privacy reasons, says that the support Coop gave her was overwhelming — in a good way. It was like having family in the courtroom with her, comforting her.

Testifying in a sexual assault case can be profoundly distressing, especially during cross-examination. Coop's warm, friendly presence would be a tremendous comfort. She's also helped children who've survived heinous crimes, including one who had never told an adult precisely what happened to her. She had been coming into counselling for weeks but, until the day Coop turned up, she had been utterly mute. When she saw Coop, she lay down on the ground, lifted up the labrador's floppy dog ear and told her what had happened. That little girl had lost her capacity to trust human beings, but she still had it in her to trust a dog. Coop, meanwhile, will not judge her, react poorly, say something inappropriate or victim-blame. She is an unconditionally loving companion who provides something humans sometimes can't.

Australians have increasingly embraced the idea of having a dog available in court, which is promising. In 2018, a Melbourne magistrate ruled that complainants in the committal hearing for Cardinal George Pell's case could have the option of taking a court support dog in with them. The accusers gave evidence by video link to the court, and they were allowed to have a support person and a support dog, if they felt like it could help. It's a tremendous kindness to give these unspeakably courageous people the chance to have company, comfort and support, right when they need it most.

In America, several states have made legislative change to give people the right to have a court support dog by their side while they attend a trial. There were objections to this, with some lawyers suggesting that seeing a cute dog standing beside someone might make that person more appealing to a jury and therefore potentially influence the verdict. In 2013, during a case in Washington's Supreme Court, it was ruled that the presence of a dog was not in fact prejudicial. A lovely dog by the name of Ellie, who actually belonged to a prosecutor working on the case, was permitted to attend trial, setting a nice precedent for others who wish to work in the law.

There's some evidence to suggest that when a specially trained dog accompanies a child into a courtroom while they give their testimony, it helps that child articulate better what they went through. It's that improved mental clarity we've heard about, perhaps, or just the comfort of a canine friend right when you need one. It also reduces the likelihood of a victim or witness being re-traumatised by having to go over in court what happened to them. That's one of the greatest concerns we have about people who have to testify: that speaking about what they went through may in fact cause them to go through the trauma of it all over again. Experts say that having these dogs in a setting like a courtroom tempers that. It can also protect police officers and other staff from going through vicarious trauma. The presence of a calm, non-judgmental animal can have a seriously soothing effect on everyone affected. Forgive me for this, but you could call it 'paw and order'.

All of this just takes us back to what we already know about dogs and, in particular, their remarkable capacity for stress relief in their human companions. When people are feeling stress of any kind, they produce more cortisol.

When we're upset and distressed, we also tend to experience increased heart rate and higher blood pressure. All of these things can affect a person's capacity to function — and certainly their ability to testify in a court of law. It can make them feel unwell and unstable and flustered. It can make them feel frightened and confused and overwhelmed. It can also affect memory, communication skills and focus, which are all things we rely on to be able to articulate a traumatic experience in a legal setting.

Ideally, a victim or witness would be calm and comfortable in front of prosecutors, defenders, judges and juries. Only then do they truly get the best possible chance to represent themselves. We know that being in the company of a dog is profoundly calming. Touching them or even just seeing them can lower our blood pressure, slow our heart rate and discourage the production of cortisol. Perhaps our greatest aid in preparing people for court, then, is to give them a canine companion for the day.

Having met Gwen, I can absolutely see how her presence on a horrifically stressful day could make a very real difference to your mood and even to your capacity to do what's required of you in court. She's a lively, friendly dog, but she can also be extremely placid. It's a magical combination of traits that makes her ideal for this profession. She and her handler, Julie, do important work every Tuesday morning. So do all the other dogs who visit courts around the world. I hope we might get to such a level of acceptance and tolerance and empathy, and see enough success in these court dog programs, that we give all survivors and witnesses of crime the opportunity to spend time with a pup like Gwen. It could truly make their experience of court less harrowing than it has to be, and that can only be a wonderful thing.

CHAPTER 9

Sir Jack Spratticus, the dog who helps with PTSD

WE ALL DESERVE A childhood. We deserve the joy and abandon of being little human beings. We deserve unconditional love and tenderness from our parents. We deserve to feel safe and comfortable and seen. Vanessa Holbrow didn't get any of those things. For Vanessa, known as Ness, growing up was about danger and fear and pain. She was assaulted, in many ways, by the very people who ought to have been looking after her. Her childhood wasn't about games and toys and imagination;

it was about surviving physical, emotional and sexual abuse. It was about learning to stay alive and stay quiet, from around the time she was learning to walk and talk. Such unimaginable trauma can take a lifetime to repair, if it's even possible for a person to completely heal.

Ness is 48 years old now. She has spent decades trying to salvage a life for herself; one she feels is worth living. She's lived with disordered eating (anorexia and bulimia) since she was 12 years old, and she lives with complex post-traumatic stress disorder (also referred to as complex trauma, abbreviated to cPTSD). She was misdiagnosed as having borderline personality disorder for several decades, and now, after personal research and independent assessments with trauma specialists, she believes she lives with something called dissociative identity disorder.

Dissociative identity disorder used to be known as having 'multiple personalities' or 'split personality disorder' (you may recall the illness was the butt of all the jokes in Jim Carrey's 2000 movie *Me, Myself and Irene*). It's a difficult condition to explain, but far more difficult, of course, to live and breathe. It basically means that Ness never had the chance to develop a real sense of identity. She never learned that she mattered. The different facets of her personality never had time to consolidate and to come together to form one person. Her development was so violently disrupted as a child that she never really got to work out who she is in this world. Her identity is fractured and there are multiple iterations of Vanessa. She flits between these personalities even now, sometimes feeling like a child, sometimes an adult, never a fully realised human being who knows herself. The many versions of Ness are different ages and different temperaments. Some of them remember what happened to her as a child and a teenager, some of them do not. She cannot predict or control when she will oscillate between these versions of herself; she simply finds herself behaving differently, holding onto a different set of memories and trying to find her way in the world each day. It is a devastating way to be.

She has visceral flashbacks and harrowing, lucid nightmares through the night, which have her changing pyjamas often and pacing her little apartment. She is tormented by what happened to her, without always being able to remember precisely what it was. She doesn't always have visual memories to attach to the sensations she's feeling; she simply knows that the trauma of her past is visiting her. Trauma is sneaky and complicated like that. Ness's mind has willed her to forget a lot of what happened as a child, but her body remembers the trauma. She feels it in her bones and the sinews of her muscles; it aches when she tries to hold onto a single memory.

Without warning, she can find herself in a state of sheer terror, as if she is fighting or begging for her life. She says it can feel, all of a sudden, like she knows she's going to die. It's that fight-or-flight reaction happening in her body, even when there is no current or imminent danger. She is simply remembering, with her whole being, what it was like to fear for her life as a child. She feels helpless and terrified, all over again, sometimes when she is simply at home doing nothing or trying to sleep. It's a perilous existence, then, always half-expecting to feel terror out of nowhere.

Ness dissociates, too. She slips out of reality for a time, forgetting where she is or what she's doing. Like dipping into a daydream, only not so nice. It's sort of like that feeling when you get in the car and you drive somewhere, and once you're there you realise, with a shock, that you have no idea how you got there. You can't remember the journey. It's like that, she says, only more like you've ducked out of your own existence for a moment and come back not really knowing who you are or what's going on. It's frightening and disorienting. It's isolating, because she often cannot explain what's just happened or where her mind went.

Dissociating began as a coping mechanism for surviving trauma when Ness was a kid. She couldn't handle the full horror of what was happening to her: it was too traumatic for one person to bear. So she'd disappear for a while, simply check out of reality and mentally switch off to protect herself. It was effective, back then, as a way to remove herself from the situation, pretend nothing bad was happening, and dilute the pain she was going through; but now it's become a problem. Now that she's trying to run a functional adult life, it's inconvenient. It's stopping her from doing ordinary everyday things and feeling in command of her own attention. So she's having to try to unlearn it, in order to cut down the time in her life that she feels confused and disoriented.

Ness hurts herself often. For years, she was in and out of hospital every month, having overdosed. Physical pain seemed to be easier to handle than the emotional turmoil. She has lasting physical damage from those attempts on her life. She also has burn marks across the skin on all her limbs, but she doesn't fully remember actually doing anything to get them. She may not know who she is, but that doesn't stop Ness from feeling guilty and ashamed and frightened of herself and what she's been through. Sustained, prolonged childhood trauma tricks people into feeling shame for acts they had no power to stop.

It can also leave a person alone and totally detached from their sense of self. As children, we're meant to bond with our parents and family members — that early attachment is monumentally important for our development as human beings. It's really what makes us the people we become, those early attachments. It's what dictates the way we interact with other people for the rest of our lives, the relationships we're able to build, and the capacity we have for things like love and trust and faith in humanity. Ness did not get that; she has never properly bonded with another human being in her life. Never fully trusted anyone, never wholly loved anyone.

Worse, she was betrayed, belittled and attacked by the very people who should have been caring for her. That aching injustice in her life has left her unsure about how she is meant to exist in this world. She doesn't always know how to interact with other people, although I have to say, in my experience, she is miraculously delightful. The fact that she manages to be so kind and sweet and curious and gentle is astounding — and a remarkable testament to her resilience as a person.

Ness used to walk along the beach near her home a lot, on her own. She doesn't find joy often in this life, but the salty air and the sand between her toes made her feel like she was alive. Sometimes she'd see dogs on her walks and she'd notice, just for a moment, the happiness they made her feel. She'd see one scamper by and she'd smile. She'd lean down to pat one on the head and she'd leave feeling cheerier. Eventually, Ness decided it might be time to get a dog for herself, so that she could hopefully feel that way every day.

She wanted to be prepared, though, because caring for a living creature is a massive responsibility, especially for someone who routinely loses the ability to care for herself. She started going to dog-training lessons on her own, just so she could learn how to treat a pup when she got one. She remembered that her grandparents had a terrier called Benjy, and that she used to burst into tears whenever she'd been around to visit him and they had to leave. So she contacted an organisation called Border Terrier Welfare in the hope of perhaps getting a dog that might help her recall one of her few happy memories.

Seven years ago, Ness brought home the dog who would change her life.

His name was originally Jack Spratticus. Ness named him after the nursery rhyme character Jack Sprat, with an added suffix just for fun. Some dogs are simply born to have surnames and Jack is one such dog. He was knighted, some years later, by a group of fellow border terriers and their people, who are members of a Twitter group called BTposse. He was receiving recognition for his noble acts as a doggy companion, as he should. So he is now known as Sir Jack Spratticus. The first of his name, king of treats, lord of the afternoon nap.

He is eight years old now, and a handsome fellow with wiry, biscuit-coloured hair all over his stout body, black, triangular ears and a greying snout. He's a compact little beast, who moves briskly and purposefully as he goes about his day. His favourite thing is going on long walks along the beach, exactly where Ness used to go and admire other people's dogs. It is her greatest joy, now, to have her own.

Ness adopted Sir Jack when he was 13 months old. He had not exactly had a happy life until that point, either. By the time she scooped him up and brought him back to her flat, he had already lived in three separate homes. He was a bit of a brute back then; vicious with other dogs, and quite fond of sinking his gnarly little teeth into human flesh. He was unwanted, as so many difficult canine characters are. Each family who took him in did so with the best of intentions, but ultimately they just couldn't deal with such a badly behaved mutt. And so he kept being rehomed, without anyone truly taking the time to teach him how to behave. He hadn't been socialised with other dogs, as all pups should be, so he just felt threatened and got ferocious whenever he met someone new.

When Ness first took Sir Jack home, she knew immediately that he'd be hard work. He used to latch his jaws onto her leg and refuse to let go. He was so aggressive with other dogs that it was impossible to take him out in public. So she set about trying to fix him. She got advice from a dog trainer, and together they worked on his behaviour until he was better. The improvements came not only from this training, but also probably from the stability of staying in one place for an extended period of time. Even so, it took Sir Jack a full year to calm down enough to really be a proper, loving pet.

Now? You should see him! He is the picture of obedience. He is dignified and calm. You can scarcely imagine how he could possibly have been anything but perfectly behaved. He's an immensely good, gentle, well-behaved and even-tempered boy. These days, he would absolutely never be seen chomping down on any person or dog. He even wins competitions for his exemplary behaviour and his notable contribution to society.

He won a special award at Crufts in 2018, which is the most auspicious dog show in the world. Geri Horner (Ginger Spice of the Spice Girls) presented him with his precious award, which he got because of the care he takes in looking after Ness as well as all his charity work. His prize is called 'The Kennel Club's Friends for Life', and it is awarded to the dog who demonstrates the most remarkable companionship and support to a human being. He has won countless other prizes for being such a good and helpful boy. His walls are now absolutely covered in rosettes and ribbons from various contests.

Sir Jack even appears as Mr October in a calendar of friendliest dog faces for the year 2018, and as Mr April for 2019. He is practically always having his photo taken, because he is such a revered little beast. He's a bit famous now, too, because television crews like to come along and hear from Ness about how he's changed her life.

Sir Jack's transformation from bad boy to best boy came about really because of Ness's diligence. She committed to making this pup better — and it worked. It's a testament to perseverance and love, that such an unruly creature could become so utterly serene and well behaved. For the first few years of Sir Jack's life he just lived as a normal pet. He accompanied Ness on long walks through the countryside, tottered merrily about their apartment and wrestled with his many toys.

By his sixth birthday, Ness had made the decision to try to get him trained up to qualify as her mental health assistance dog. That would mean he could legally accompany her anywhere, which would help with her social anxiety. She got in touch with an organisation called Canine Generated Independence, which helps people who live with invisible disabilities train their dogs. Each pup has to be extremely obedient. To qualify for their mental health assistance jacket, they must be able to demonstrate that they can perform at least three tasks that make their human's life easier, safer and better.

So, after much hard work and training, Sir Jack learned to behave. Not just behave, but actively help Ness when she needs him. He can now fetch the landline phone and bring it to Ness if she is in any way incapacitated. All she needs to say is the word 'call' and he will scamper along their living-room floor, pick the phone up in his mouth and deliver it to her, wherever she is. She can then call emergency services or a friend who might be able to help her out of whatever state or crisis she's in. He can also fetch her medication for her. They agreed on the command being 'find green' because Ness keeps the medication she takes in a green zip-up case, just the right size and shape to be carried by one Sir Jack. When she says those words, he will search for that bag and get it to her, promptly. It doesn't matter where the bag is hiding in the apartment — and it moves around a lot — he will locate it and bring it to Ness.

He can also provide deep pressure, which means he has been trained to lie across Ness's body and use his weight to calm her down when she is panicky or having an anxiety attack. If she lies down, he can tell the difference between an innocent nap and an act of desperation. He knows what her anxiety attacks look like, and he simply goes about the business of soothing her. He can also startle her out of a dissociative state and snap her out of a flashback. When they're out and about, Sir Jack can also be summoned by a call to come and stand between Ness's legs. This has a calming effect, for times when she cannot lie down. Having him stand by her like that is immensely reassuring, and grounds her when she starts to feel uneasy or frightened.

Bless him, he can also unload the laundry from the washing machine, although Ness says she doesn't ask him to do that often. If he does that, it's really just to show off. He also obviously knows the basic stuff, like how to sit and stay and come to his name. He's a very clever little bloke, and he makes Ness's life significantly easier to live. She feels safer, knowing that he can intervene if she can't get to the phone or reach her medication. She feels calmer, knowing she can simply ask for a restorative snuggle and she'll get one.

Apart from these very nifty tricks, Sir Jack also provides tremendous companionship. He is Ness's closest friend, her confidant and her ally. He is her carer and she is his. They both had rough beginnings in life, but they've found each other and settled into a relatively peaceful existence side by side.

Ness still has an enormous amount of work to do in therapy, to dissuade her from dissociating, to coax her back into eating solid food and to stop her from wanting to hurt herself. She has so much left to understand about herself and, really, she still needs to work out how to reconcile all those different facets of her personality so that she can have some idea of who she is now. She says that Sir Jack gives her the desire and the motivation to do that. He gives her self-esteem and purpose and a reason to live. She finds it much harder to hurt herself, she says, because what would her little mate do if something happened to her? Being responsible for Sir Jack's welfare has made an enormous difference in Ness's life. It has made her feel worthy and important and needed. It's the first time she's felt emotionally attached to a living being. She cannot overstate how vital and restorative and wonderful that has been for her. It's what she's been craving all these decades, and here it is, in the stout form of a border terrier.

When I visited Ness and Sir Jack, I am so touched by the relationship they have. I could see that it was special immediately. As I got off the train, I saw Sir Jack standing proudly at Ness's feet. Ness was nervous but also tentatively excited that day, because she sensed that I would be a safe person to speak to and she really wants her story to be told. She's angry and sad and desperate to fight for the help she needs — and she thinks that if she entrusts her story to someone outside her normal life, she might have some better hope of people understanding what a profound effect childhood trauma can have on a person forever.

We hop into Ness's bubble car, and I'm told I must sit in the back seat because Sir Jack is used to being up front in the passenger seat, beside Ness. He sits pertly in a bed that's been strapped into the front and watches out the window in case something needs to be barked at. Ness drives us gingerly back to her home, where we sit and drink tea while she tries to piece together her story.

Ness's apartment is a joy to behold. She and Sir Jack live on the first floor of an apartment block, in a small, completely enchanting flat. There are paintings, sketches and photographs of Sir Jack on just about every possible inch of wall space. Everywhere you look, his face is staring back at you. I'd say there could easily be 60 pieces of artwork starring Sir Jack in the apartment, perhaps more. I get the feeling it's not complete yet either. Ness simply continues to collect pictures of her beloved dog; sometimes by friends, often by strangers who offer to paint or sketch him. She has positive affirmations ('You are enough' and 'Home is where your dog is') pinned to the walls, too. She has ornaments and trinkets, mostly dog-themed, on just about every available surface. And of course the many awards Sir Jack has won.

In the kitchen, living room and bedroom, she has hung pastel-coloured bunting across the space and slung different-coloured fairy lights from wall to wall. It is a dreamy space. I find myself thinking that this is probably how I would've decorated my home if I'd had one as a child or a teenager. Ness says the child version of herself was really in charge of the décor. I am pleased to know that she lives in this space. It feels safe and comforting and feminine and sweet.

Over the course of several hours, Ness tries to explain to me what Sir Jack has done for her. She is so proud of him — and tentatively hopeful about her future, when she can *be*, because he has given her the confidence to be. She finds it difficult to concentrate long enough to complete some thoughts, and at times I'm scared that I've asked too much of her. Telling her story and boasting about her wonderful dog seems to make Ness happy, though, and I am honoured that she let me tell some of it here.

I think about Ness often now, and we exchange photos of our dogs fairly regularly. I am always pleased when a beautiful picture of Sir Jack pops up in my WhatsApp. They are a truly special pair, these two, and I am lucky to have met them. I can only hope and wish that Ness is able to get more of the help she needs to continue getting better. It is a comfort to know that Sir Jack will be there while she tries to piece together who she is and what she wants from this life.

*

It is remarkable to witness how helpful a dog can be for someone living with a severe psychiatric illness. Thankfully, I'm not the only person who's seen the effect a dog can have on someone who needs love and support. Psychiatric and mental health assistance dogs are becoming more popular around the world. The more we speak to people about their experiences with these specially trained pups, the more we understand how wonderfully helpful and potentially life-changing their presence can be. We already know how much a dog can affect someone's physical health, by lowering their blood pressure, keeping them active, mitigating their pain, making them feel calm, slowing their heart rate and triggering a surge of that precious hormone oxytocin. It shouldn't be too much of a surprise, really, that those things might improve a person's mental health, too. There's an ever-expanding body of research that backs up our more emotional and anecdotal observations about how mental health assistance dogs can help.

Associate Professor Janice Lloyd, from the Department of Veterinary Sciences at James Cook University in Queensland, Australia, and her team, conducted a survey with 199 people who own mental health assistance dogs in Australia. They all responded to an extensive survey about the breed of dog they have, the type of training they underwent, and the benefits they experience as a result of that human–dog bond. They partnered with an organisation called mindDog, which helps people with a disability or a mental illness train dogs to qualify as their assistance animals.

The majority (84 per cent) of respondents needed an assistance dog to help them mitigate symptoms of depression. Sixty per cent had an anxiety disorder, 62 per cent had PTSD, and 57 per cent reported that they had panic attacks. The most common task these people asked their dogs to perform was reducing their anxiety through tactile stimulation — that is, physical contact like stroking or cuddling. Ninety-four per cent of people require cuddles to quell their anxiety, which is unsurprising to me because I know the power of a dog hug. Seventy-one per cent said they need their dogs to nudge or paw them in order to bring them back to the present, which is particularly helpful for hallucinations, moments of dissociation and panic attacks. Fifty-one said they need their dogs to interrupt an undesirable behaviour state, which might be anxiety, anger, panic or distress of some sort. It may also be self-harm, bingeing, purging or putting themselves in danger. Forty-five per cent of people, so just under half, require deep pressure stimulation, which is when the pup uses their body weight to calm and soothe a person.

Forty-two per cent of respondents noted that they need their dogs to block contact from other people, which helps in the instance of social anxiety or fear in public places. Otherwise, people who responded to this survey said they benefited from having an assistance dog because the dog: forced them to leave the house (which they may not do on their own); reminded them to take their medication; kept them safe; and gave them a reality-check when they disassociated from real life.

This study also revealed that 46 per cent of people paid fewer visits to psychiatric and other healthcare centres when they had a dog. That was mainly because they made fewer suicide attempts, had fewer times when they needed to be hospitalised, and had a reduced need for medication. Conversely, 30 per cent actually reported an increase in the use of psychiatric and healthcare services since getting an assistance dog, which is explained by the fact that they felt more confident and able to leave the house, go out in public and actually attend their medical appointments. Either way, that's a lot of lives significantly changed by the presence of a well-behaved mutt.

It's also interesting to note which sorts of dogs became mental health assistance dogs. Most people suspect that they've got to be specially bred labradors and golden retrievers. Those breeds of dog are obviously magnificent, and we already know they make perfect guide dogs and therapy dogs. What this study revealed, though, is that any dog can be trained to become a mental health assistance dog. Any shape, any size, any breed, from the chihuahua to the Irish wolfhound. Encouragingly, a full fifth of these dogs came from rescue shelters, which tells us something we already know: that dogs from rescue shelters are perfectly capable of being tamed and loved into good behaviour. Every single response to the question 'What does your dog mean to you?' was positive, without exception. For every breed and for all rescue pups.

The only real negative that came from the survey was that the respondents don't believe that public perception has caught up with the necessity and importance of these types of assistance animals. They reported that it can be stressful to take their dog out in public, and into businesses and places where normally dogs are not allowed, because strangers would challenge them on their right to be there with a dog. Most people are well aware of guide dogs for the blind and deaf, and you can usually tell if someone has that sort of disability, so it's easier to appreciate the presence of a dog who can help. With an invisible illness like depression, anxiety or PTSD, it's much more difficult to instantly recognise why a person might need a dog. Many people simply do not know about the existence of mental health assistance dogs. There's also the added stigma that's attached to mental health problems, meaning people might be less likely to explain the real reason they have a dog with them. That's a problem that really needs to be addressed. Hopefully, as more and more people apply to have these sorts of dogs and medical professionals start to prescribe pets as therapy, we'll get a surge in awareness and therefore sensitivity towards people who need their pups to escort them everywhere.

We cannot cure a mental illness by giving someone a dog for a housemate. We cannot take away or disappear the trauma that stays with someone their whole life just by giving them some canine company. That sort of recuperation can take a lifetime of therapy, medication and other treatment — help that an astonishing number of people cannot or do not access. Mental illness doesn't generally get cured. It can be managed, though. It can be mitigated. It can be held at bay, or contained as much as humanly possible, to allow a person to live their life as best they can. It can be tamed, to a certain extent, but it cannot be erased. That's something each person who lives with a mental health problem comes to understand, as they get older: that perhaps they can live stretches of their life uninterrupted by trauma or depression or anxiety, but ultimately that condition will most likely be a companion to them for the rest of their time on Earth. Really, all we can do is fight it the best we can, seek the best help we can get, hope for an improvement in our access to treatment, and do whatever the bloody hell we can to cheer ourselves up in the meantime.

I hope scientists will come up with ever better treatments for mental illness, and I hope our policy-makers will do us the courtesy of supplying affordable healthcare to everyone who needs it. In the meantime, while we keep fighting to stay alive, to love, to function and to live, we may as well be spending our precious time with creatures who make us feel necessary and loved and at peace with ourselves. That's what I want for

Ness: the longest possible time on this planet with her darling companion, Sir Jack Spratticus. That's what I want for anyone who has discovered the joys and comforts of having a pup in their lives. Maybe it won't work for everyone, maybe there are people who would prefer a cat, maybe there are people who are immune to the charms of an animal. I don't know. But I do know what it's like to live in distress and lose control of your own emotions.

I may not know the trauma Ness has known in her life, but I'd like to think I understand it a little more since having met her. I have seen Ness with her beloved dog, and I know that he is one of the reasons she is still alive. May they — and every other human–dog best friend duo — live happily together as long as they can. May they walk and cuddle and eat and nap together for years to come. May they find what anyone who's known emotional distress really needs: peace and quiet and rest and contentedness.

CHAPTER 10

Teddy, the dog who woke his owner from a coma

ANDY SZASZ IS A 65-year-old male human being. Average height, pale skin, graphite-coloured hair in sharpish peaks on the top of his head. When he turns up at the train station to meet me, he's dressed head-to-toe in shades of red wine: burgundy shirt, maroon shorts, indigo sneakers. He's standing with his greatest companion in the world, a sweet, medium-sized dog known as a schnoodle because he is part schnauzer, part poodle. His name is Teddy; or Ted, for short, once you get to know him. He's black all over, almost silver when the sun catches his coat, except near his snout, where his beard melts into a slight chocolate colour. He's got glossy, brown-black eyes, with a thin, roving sliver of white that appears when he looks around.

Andy's got Teddy on a short lead, and he's sitting ever so neatly at his owner's ankles, waiting for me to come through the gate. You can tell immediately, just from looking at him, that his manners are impeccable. Teddy trots along next to us through the car park, and all three of us bundle into Andy's car, with the four-legged among us displaced from the usual spot in the passenger's seat onto a plump little pillow in the back.

Teddy sits quietly, politely, on his quilted throne while Andy gives me a tour of Southampton, on England's south coast. Andy's been here his whole life, and, if he hadn't worked 14-hour days as a civil engineer for the decades of his career, he could've had a nice side hustle as a tour guide. He gestures out the window as we glide along: over here is a noteworthy pub, over there is a spanking-new Westfield shopping centre. Over here are the remnants of a grand castle, over there is the museum with an interactive replica of the *Titanic*. This is of course the city from which the *Titanic* so confidently set out to sea early last century; a somewhat awkward point of pride for the city's residents, given the almighty ship's unfortunate run-in with an iceberg in April 1912. Still, a city must claim its history and this one does. Andy continues: to our right is where he once lived, to our left is the university, which explains why so many of the people wandering these streets look 19 years old.

On the way to his place, Andy warns me about the current state of his beloved home. Here is a man who has nearly completed the gargantuan task of packing his life's belongings neatly into piles of boxes, having finally settled a rather messy divorce, some 18 months after his now ex-wife moved out.

When we arrive, it's to an almost empty house. The kitchen still has a fridge, a kettle and the ingredients for two mugs of warm, milky tea. The floor is covered in cardboard boxes, not yet sticky-taped shut, perhaps awaiting further contents. There are old recipe books that belonged to Andy's mother nestled in among Enid Blyton books he must have read aloud to all of his four sons, now aged between 24 and 39.

In the living room, which looks out onto a rather lovely garden, there are two beige chairs sat next to one another, waiting for us. There's a scattering of cosy-looking blankets on the floor, where Teddy is welcome to settle for one of his many daily naps. He lies down by the door as we sit down, lining his spine neatly up against the skirting-board. He's not really moved to lavish his latest visitor in kisses or cuddles. He gives us a gentle wag of his tail and proceeds to snore elegantly, with a little wrinkle of his wet nose every time he exhales. It's a familiar background noise to me, the warm snuffling of a medium-sized beast who knows his human will wake him if there are any snacks to be had.

We sit, steaming mugs in hands, and Andy tells me how Teddy came into his life, and he into Ted's. It was six and a half years ago, just about, and Andy was not meant to get a dog. He and his then wife had always had jack russell terriers, four of them in a row, one waddling into their lives after the other. Some time after the last jack russell had passed away, the sister of one of Andy's sons' girlfriends was working in an RSPCA shelter and, knowing how partial Andy is to some dog company, she invited him to come and visit her. He did, though he promised his wife he wasn't going to bring home another dog. But then, you see, when he got there, he met Ted.

Teddy, who wasn't called Teddy at the time, took an instant liking to Andy. He chose Andy, in that magical way a pup in a rescue shelter sometimes decides on their human companion. Andy didn't really have much say in the matter, truth be told. Who was he to refuse the affections of a very well-behaved schnoodle? Teddy was just 16 weeks old back then, a little hiccup of a creature, all scraggly and shaggy and warm. He put his wet nose up against Andy's shin and, to be honest, that's probably all it took to ensnare Andy. We are simple people, dog people; it doesn't take much for us to fall in love with a pup.

Teddy had been abandoned by his previous family, allegedly because one of them was allergic, but Andy is sceptical about that story, as, with their combination of hair and wool, schnoodles tend to not have the type of fur that causes allergic reactions. Rather, Andy is more inclined to believe that Ted was rambunctious, as pups can be, and the humans get overwhelmed, as they can do.

Anyway, somehow, accidentally, breaking all those sincerely doled-out promises, Andy opened his wallet, paid the adoption fee of £140 and took that handful of puppy home with him. He was named Teddy, and he immediately became a member of the family. It's important to state, for the record, that even then, according to Andy, Teddy was primarily his dog. Ever since that first snuffle against Andy's calves, he and Teddy have been as close as can be. They are man and dog, best mates, companions, allies. Which is just as well, truly, because they have needed each other these past few years. Teddy's needs have remained fairly constant: warmth and shelter and food and treats and walks and somewhere to snuggle up at night. A collection of rather nice jackets, jumpers and raincoats for all occasions, too, if you don't mind. Andy's needs, however, have been a bit more complicated.

Three months after Teddy came home with him, Andy was diagnosed with bowel cancer. He was shocked, as for the first six decades of his life Andy had been almost rudely healthy. He swears he'd barely been sick all these years, not even with a common cold. The cancer diagnosis was a nasty, frightening reminder of mortality for a man who still felt young and probably, just quietly, a bit invincible.

Andy went in for an operation and couldn't walk for ten weeks after. During that time, Teddy simply curled up on the bed beside him and wouldn't leave. It was like Teddy knew that something major had happened to Andy, because he never jumped up on him like he usually would. He just rested his head on Andy's shoulder and snoozed away the weeks it took Andy to heal. All in all, Andy was at home with Teddy for 26 weeks.

At first, Andy's wife would take Teddy for a walk each day. However, the moment he was given his doctor's blessing to walk around a bit, Andy was out the door with Ted, down to their favourite local park for an amble about. They built up strength and stamina, taking longer walks when they could. After a while, they were doing three walks a day, gently getting those lungs used to taking in the fresh sea air again. After about 14 weeks, Andy reckons they were walking at least six miles a day. Andy credits Teddy — and his need to move his paws — for his own recovered fitness after the operation.

Their gentle training regime helped Andy get his health and his confidence back. And that is the faithful two-step benefit of having a dog around when you're not feeling your best self: they'll keep you company when you need to be sedentary, and they'll get you out of the house as soon as you're capable of putting one foot in front of the other. Ted gave Andy a purpose, because he was responsible for looking after the dog. Whenever he felt bereft or alone, he'd just look down at Ted and remember why he wanted to get better. The simple pleasure of wandering around their favourite park together was enough to rouse Andy back into getting his old life back.

Once Andy was feeling up to it and he'd been given the all-clear, he returned to work — but not without his mate. Teddy was promoted to, let's say, executive assistant, even though he knew remarkably little about highway design. Andy bought his companion a hi-vis jacket, which he promptly got used to wearing every day, and they went into the office and out for site visits together. Andy's colleagues were delighted, and fought to give Teddy sneaky treats from the office biscuit tin. When Andy was sat at his desk working, Teddy would perch on a chair right beside him. If anyone went to the kitchen for a snack or a cuppa, Teddy would jump down and lope after them, just in case they needed his assistance. Their lives carried on like this — until Andy's mother had a heart attack.

It was November 2016 and the weather hadn't quite made up its mind. You could be in a T-shirt one minute and freezing cold the next. Andy flew out to Minnesota in the United States to see his mama. It was snowing there, and he'd spend all day every day by her bedside in hospital, accepting various visitors. It was there that he picked up some germs. By the time he flew back home, Andy was feeling unwell. As we've established, apart from the cancer, Andy doesn't generally get sick. However, he told his boss he needed to stay in bed a few days, and his wife rang and made him an appointment at the doctors. The moment he walked in the door and a nurse saw him, they called an ambulance immediately.

The next thing Andy remembers was lying on one of those thin, wheeled hospital beds, being pushed through ominous big silver doors. Then it's all a blank until he remembers waking up with all sorts of tubes attached to his body, helping him breathe. He had pneumonia and influenza, a double-whammy that really knocked him out. He had an operation to save him, and he stopped breathing twice. The doctors decided to put Andy in a medically induced coma.

While Andy was unconscious, his family would come and go. They'd play games at his bedside to pass the time, all the while including him in the conversation. Andy shows me a photograph of him, very much still in a coma, with a hand of cards placed carefully into his outstretched palms so it looked like he is joining in a game of gin rummy. During her visits, Andy's then wife noticed someone walking a dog around the hospital ward. Southampton General Hospital has a therapy dog program and, knowing how much Andy loves dogs, she asked if the resident pup could come for a visit.

Andy didn't notice the dog's presence, but it gave his wife an idea. She asked the head nurse if she could please bring Teddy in for a visit, even though he technically wasn't supposed to be in the hospital. The nurse agreed, because, like most nurses, she is one of the best sorts of human beings possible. Andy's wife went home and got Ted. She smuggled him into the hospital, concealing him in a giant plastic supermarket bag.

As soon as Ted saw Andy, he bounded up onto Andy's bed and licked his face, as he always does. He barked just the once, as if to say, hey, pay me some attention, old man. Then, something pretty remarkable happened. Andy woke up. The feeling of Teddy's rough tongue on his cheek and the sound of that solitary bark was enough to bring Andy back to waking life. Teddy, for his part, went mad with happiness. He wagged his tail, he jumped around, he celebrated the return of his favourite person.

The nurses and doctors could not believe it. Nobody could; it was almost beyond belief. Andy had come out of the coma four days earlier than he was meant to, all because his four-legged mate came to visit.

Andy was put in isolation for a bit longer because his influenza was so bad. But not even that was enough to keep man and dog apart, as his family would bring Teddy to the window and shake his paw to wave. The only things Andy really remembers from that groggy, foggy time were the acrid-clean hospital smell and the sight of Ted on the other side of the glass.

He was disoriented, waking up from the coma, and he did some strange drawings of things he thought he saw. One day, when one of his sons came in to visit, he saw an old man lying in the bed beside him. His son went out for 20 minutes, and when he came back the man had vanished. Andy says that was his guardian angel.

Five days after Teddy came in to wake Andy, he was back home in his own bed. And Ted, because it was just before Christmas, was sporting a new Christmas jumper. As Andy recovered, he slipped into a familiar routine: sleeping beside Ted until he was ready and able to walk around outside again. For 18 weeks he languished in bed, getting up when he could to rebuild his strength down at the dog park with his faithful hound.

It made perfect, even poetical sense, really, that Teddy was the one to wake Andy. He'd been his four-legged medical supervisor before, when Andy was battling cancer, and he was simply doing what he could to rouse his best mate again.

Andy was profoundly moved by what had happened, and made the decision to offer Teddy's services to other people who might need them. He approached the charity Pets As Therapy who ran the program in the hospital he'd been in. He registered Ted's interest and they sent out a local assessor to see if he'd be up for the job. Therapy dogs who work in hospitals have to have a particular disposition. They have to be resilient and calm, tender and patient. They have to be utterly unflappable.

The person who came to assess Teddy put him through all sorts of tests to see how he'd react. He took him for walks, threw things, made loud noises, introduced him to other dogs and took him up to different sorts of people. Teddy was resolutely unfussed by it all. He didn't bark or whimper or snarl, not once. The only thing he ever barks at, by the way, is squirrels scampering up a tree. And given that there aren't typically many tree-scampering squirrels in the wards of a general hospital, they figured he was probably going to be eminently suitable for the position.

Teddy's a bit famous now, you know. As soon as the local press heard about the brave pup who'd woken his human from a coma, they descended on the hospital to file stories. Once Ted returned to the same hospital in his new capacity as therapy dog, media from all around the world started to report on his new-found career. He's been on Italian television; he's been on Scottish radio.

Ted was given a very special award by the RSPCA, who had looked after him when he was small. He attended a red-carpet event to accept his award, but declined to make an acceptance speech. He wore one of his many bow-ties — as he does on every hospital visit. He is now an ambassador for the RSPCA, which means he has continued his work raising awareness for rescue dogs and therapy dogs. He's really a very, very good boy.

Now, Andy takes Ted into the hospital several times a week. On a typical day, they get up at 6 am. Teddy goes out into the garden for his morning wee and comes back in for a treat. He waits while Andy dresses and downs a tea. Then he bounds into the car and sits on the front seat with his head out the window, ears flapping in the breeze. They go to the park for the first walk of the day.

On hospital days, they have breakfast and then head in for three or four hours. They come in the main entrance and have to greet everyone: the women who work in the charity shop, the nurses at their station, the doctors in the staff room, the consultant who helped Andy when he was sick. They're not technically allowed to feed Teddy while he's working, but they do because all good boys deserve treats. Andy and Teddy then get a list of patients they're assigned to see that day, a lot of whom are stroke patients. They sometimes see as many as a dozen people in a day, and they always get asked for impromptu visits outside their allocated list. They're extremely popular, you have to understand. Everywhere they appear, they put a smile on someone's face, whether it's a nurse who's just worked a gruelling double-shift or an 18-year-old cancer patient who's been told she's going to die soon.

Teddy is allowed to sit on a chair beside the hospital beds or on a mat on top of the bed. He usually opts for the latter, to get closer to the person who needs the warmth of his little body on their lap. One woman, a stroke survivor, got out of bed and walked for the first time since she'd been unwell, just so she could come and greet Teddy. One man, who'd been told there was nothing more the doctors could do for him, spent his dying days with Teddy by his side.

Every single person who gets to see and pat Teddy is better for the experience. They remember what it's like to love and be loved, if that's something they've forgotten. They remember what it is to gaze into the smelly, toothy grin of a dog who just loves being around humans. They remember what pure, uncomplicated joy feels like, even if it's just a passing distraction between periods of great sadness.

On days without hospital visits, Andy might take Teddy down the pub for lunch. Andy met his best friend down at the dog park. John is 92 years old and used to be a fire-fighter during the war, so he's got stories for days. They'll take Teddy and John's dog, a Welsh collie called Buddy, out for a walk in the afternoon. They'll get an ice cream from the van that circles the area, sit on a bench and talk about their lives. Sometimes, John's wife, Marion, will make them tea. They stop and chat to the other dog walkers at the park; the easy banter of people brought together by their decision to care for a dog. Andy and Teddy will usually go for three or four walks in a day. Their lives are completely enmeshed; they spend all their time together and really, truly, are one another's great loves.

When I visit Andy and Ted, we go to the pub for baguettes lined with bacon and homemade chips. We drink ice-cold water and watch as the waitresses fawn over Teddy. He rolls over onto his back as soon as they approach, so he's in prime position for belly scratches. He waits patiently as they go behind the bar and return with a handful of treats, which they crumble for him and leave at his feet. He greets everyone who passes with the same calm but eager enthusiasm that he doles out at the hospital. He is, as most dogs are, a total joy to be around. My heart rate feels lower just being close to him, and I cannot stop looking down at him, beneath the table, just to check if he's being especially cute, which he always is.

After lunch, we're back in the car to go to the park. Andy wants me to see the important work Teddy does there:

namely, standing at the foot of one particular, thick-trunked tree, waiting for a squirrel to emerge. As soon as the car door opens, Teddy sprints across the park to the tree he believes is most likely to contain squirrels. He gets down low on the ground, maybe with a little rumble in his throat, and waits. Andy lights a cigarette and starts telling me about the rambling great hospital that used to sit on this land. He tells me about the ferries and the cruise ships that dock in at the port, like the *Titanic* once did. The whole time he keeps his eye on Ted, though, with a serious glint of love in that eye.

Andy tells me repeatedly throughout my visit that Teddy is his life. 'He's my whole life,' he says, again and again. I believe it, too. I see it. Where loneliness might have sneaked into Andy's heart and taken up residence, there is mostly patient, lovely joy. Andy and Teddy have their routine: walk, hospital, walk, pub, walk, ice cream, walk, home, repeat. Andy sees one of his sons for dinner every Tuesday night, he's got friends to visit in London and he's got his best mates from the dog park. He's got plans to travel, maybe get a campervan and go to the Lake District. But most of all, he's got Ted. Wherever he goes, whatever he does, however close he gets to death, Teddy is right there by his side.

And how generous, too, to know Teddy's capacity to help a person heal and to decide to offer his services to other people who might need it. Andy's choice to take Teddy into Southampton Hospital to visit strangers is kind — and you can just imagine the effect they have, walking in there together, sitting by people who need the company and the cuddles and the solace. It's a pleasure for Andy, and a transformative delight for everyone else.

*

A volunteer nearby at Southampton Children's Hospital, a woman called Lyndsey Uglow, was so moved by her experience taking her golden retriever to see sick kids that she decided to study its effect. She now has a Certificate for Animal Assisted Therapy, Activities and Learning from the University of Denver. To quantify how important these dog visits can be to kids and their families, Lyndsey made a survey available to all parents and staff at the children's hospital. Two hundred people filled it in and returned it. One hundred per cent of those people recommended that dog therapy programs be rolled out across the UK, which is a pretty startling endorsement. Ninety-six per cent said they had no concerns about seeing a dog on the wards at their hospital, and 95 per cent said there was no disruption caused (the remaining 5 per cent ticked 'hardly at all').

Parents and staff reported that they'd seen young patients who were able to get an MRI without anaesthesia and go into the operating theatre without sedation, purely because they'd spent time with a dog beforehand and it had calmed them enough to go through with the upcoming procedure unaided. Ninety-eight per cent of parents said the visit from a dog was 'very worthwhile'. There were no complaints about the cleanliness or behaviour of the six golden retrievers who visit that hospital. If there were, they could have been reassured that each dog is impeccably behaved, they sit on a plastic sheet to prevent direct contact with bedding, and everyone religiously uses antiseptic handwash after a visit.

The dogs — Milo, Hattie, Quinn, Jessie, Leo and Archie — are always gentle, patient and sweet. They know they're doing important work when they're in the hospital, so they save any chasing or barking or other doggish behaviours for outside, in their own time. Often, when they're working, they'll do very brave and helpful things, like demonstrate how to get an X-ray or lie on a particular machine, so that kids can watch them and see that the procedure they're about to go in for isn't as scary as they might have first thought. The dogs escort kids to chemotherapy, let them hold a paw during blood tests, and pop up on a bed for belly scratches to defuse any tension in the room. While they're on the job, they wear very sweet, bright turquoise harnesses to indicate that they're therapy dogs at the hospital. They are very, very good boys and girls.

Meanwhile, in America, researchers conducted a study to test the hypothesis that visits from a dog can decrease pain, respiratory rate and negative moods, as well as encouraging a lift in energy levels. Nurses would take a patient's blood pressure and measure their respiratory rate before and after a ten-minute visit from a dog, a couple of times a week for several months. The nurses would also help the patients fill in surveys, where they rated themselves on things like pain, anxiety, tension, depression and energy levels.

After a review of 59 patients, ranging from 24 to 88 years old and having been in the hospital between one and 60 days, they found that spending even that small amount of time with a dog caused a significant decrease in perceived pain, anxiety and depression. Mood disturbance scores decreased by 57 per cent, which is a remarkable result. People reported significant drops in tension, anger and fatigue. Blood pressure and respiratory rates were also down — only a bit, but still noticeable. Patients reported having more energy after seeing the dogs. They also used words like 'calming', 'nice', 'comforting' and 'relaxing' to describe the effect that seeing a dog had on them. There were no negative comments recorded about the experience of having a dog visit during a stay in hospital.

There were several very sweet handwritten notes returned with the survey, one of which said: 'I thought that I would not smile today, and then I saw Maggie!' Maggie was, of course, the dog chosen to visit that day. A respite in an otherwise agonising and potentially frightening experience.

Some of the patients participating in this survey were diagnosed with cancer, AIDS and heart disease. Others were recovering from operations like a hysterectomy, amputation and bypass surgery. Whatever ailed them, they had ten minutes of relief with a dog, the effects of which extended beyond their departure from the hospital.

It's particularly fascinating to consider the effect of a decrease in stress, because we know how harmful that nasty stress hormone cortisol can be. Doctors say that things like reduced anxiety, weakened depression and suspended panic can have a very profound effect on someone's capacity to recover. Psychological stress can impede the immune system and significantly slow down the body's recovery rate, so it is quite wonderful if we can find simple, happy ways to inspire that change in people. It's also enormously encouraging that people felt like they had more energy after being visited by a canine companion.

Hospital is not exactly a joyous place — except, perhaps, the maternity ward. If you're languishing in a hospital bed for any length of time, recuperating from an illness or an injury or an operation, it's usually quite unpleasant. You're managing pain, you're anxious about results, you're scared. You're away from your family, in a deeply unfamiliar place, without any of your usual comforts. You're in a thin, unfriendly bed with bright lights above, with perhaps a television for company and the arrival of three miserable-looking meals a day. Sleep does not come easily. It can be a disconcerting, frightening, even traumatising time.

Imagine, then, how you'd feel when a dog came in to see you. Imagine seeing Quinn the impeccable golden retriever or Teddy the valiant schnoodle scampering politely down the corridor towards you, dropping by your room for a cuddle before moving on to bring happiness to other patients. It would be such a welcome disruption; a moment of joy and warmth and love to help push into the background all the other unpleasantness that comes with being in a hospital. As we know now, it can also have very real positive physiological and psychological effects.

When Andy was in hospital, Ted just about saved his life. He woke him from a coma and then sat by him at home while he recovered. He has been Andy's primary companion on this planet every day since. He's a miraculous little creature — sweet, patient, well behaved, affectionate and brave. He has infinitely improved Andy's life, and he knows it. This happens, in smaller bursts, for people in hospitals, too.

Whether it's ten minutes or a whole canine lifetime that you get to spend with a dog, they can utterly change the way you approach each day of your life. They can make you feel physically and mentally stronger, even if it's only for a moment, at what might be some of the most challenging or frightening times in your life. Or they can simply make you smile on a day when you didn't think smiling would be possible. Bless them, these precious munchkins who live among us and roam our hospital hallways, just trying to help us get better. Shower them in treats, pat their hairy heads and let them nap heartily — because they deserve it.

CHAPTER 11

Noodle, the dog who works in dementia wards

NOODLE IS A SCHNOODLE. Part schnauzer, part poodle. She's Noodle the schnoodle, which is a pleasing title for a creature. It makes you feel faintly ridiculous to say it aloud, and yet, when you've done it once, you'll want to do it again. It has a nice sort of Dr Seuss vibe to it.

Noodle (the schnoodle) is nine years old, tottering towards a decade, and her wet, black, button nose would just about reach your knee if she was sitting beside you. She's a darkish grey all over, with slightly lighter patches, almost white, almost silver, on the ends of her paws, in her beard and on her chin. She looks up at you with bright, hopeful black eyes, past shaggy tufts of hair on the top of her head that you might call eyebrows. They're slightly lighter than the rest of her body too, which gives her a distinguished look, like she might be elderly or wise. She wears a smart red leather collar with a silver, bone-shaped name tag dangling from it. Her little body is strapped into a sensible royal blue harness, attached to which is a thick black lead, connecting her to the human being she follows around the most.

Deborah Taffler, Debbie, spends most of her days in extremely close proximity to Noodle. She's a marketing consultant (Debbie, not Noodle) and will take her eminent-looking dog with her to as many client meetings as she can wrangle. They've been living together for almost all of Noodle's life — all except the first six months of the dog's time on this planet.

When Noodle was born, she was bought from a breeder by a couple, as a gift for their young daughter. Generally speaking, though, dogs do not make terribly successful gifts. There's something about the act of presenting them as an object to delight someone that makes them seem disposable, or just for pleasure, when in fact they are a considerable financial, emotional and temporal commitment. Like other gifts, dogs are very often returned or abandoned when the recipient tires of playing with them. This is why dog shelters and rescue centres the world over are teeming with neglected pups; creatures who've so often been bought with the sweetest of intentions, only to be discarded when they don't quite fit into the celebrated person's life as neatly or as obediently as expected.

Most gifts do not grumble, bite, snore, wee on the carpet or chew furniture, you see, so they're easier to assimilate into your life or simply re-gift to someone else. Dogs, being living creatures, are somewhat more demanding than a book, a gift voucher or a bottle of prosecco. They're gifts that stay in your life for many years, if you're lucky. They're gifts that require feeding and cleaning and walking.

The couple who gave Noodle her first home had bought their son a Staffordshire bull terrier — a staffie — five years earlier. The staffie was quite likeable on his own, as they tend to be. Despite their reputation, staffies can have extremely sweet temperaments and be very gentle with children. Like any other dog, though, this one wasn't sure about having a new housemate. Tiny, female schnoodles, for example. The moment Noodle was brought into this family's home, their staffie got territorial. When a new dog is introduced to a home, they should really meet any existing pets beforehand, and on neutral territory, so they get off to a good start. The couple's solution to this conflict was to lock Noodle in the kitchen — permanently. She cowered in a bed between the dishwasher and the washing machine, where she'd try to get some sleep despite the vibrations from both. She was let out in the garden to wee, but otherwise stayed captive in that kitchen. Noodle got very thin and was perpetually scared.

After half a year of her living in constant fear, the family housing Noodle contacted a rescue centre to see if they could find her a more suitable home. The centre phoned Debbie, who'd spent months searching for a cross-breed rescue puppy who didn't shed. Her husband is a doctor, who was very much into the idea of getting a dog but had put in a request for a non-shedding pup so that he could turn up to his clinic without being covered head-to-toe in dog hair. And so Debbie was invited to visit Noodle in her kitchen home, to see whether they'd get on. Debbie estimates that it took all of 30 seconds before she was besotted and completely ready to pop Noodle into her car and drive her directly home forever.

It took about three months for Noodle to feel safe again. She was terrified of all other dogs and she didn't like being left on her own. Now, she's always pleased to meet other dogs and will politely greet them with a sniff and a gentle wag of the tail.

When Debbie, Noodle and I meet, at a dog-friendly café that serves excellent shakshuka, Noodle waggles her bottom excitedly every time another hound walks through the door. She pricks her ears up when two babies under the age of one sit beside us, but otherwise she simply sits at our feet, snoozing and watching the waitstaff's feet go by. She's the sort of dog you could almost mistake for being boring; purely because she's so well behaved, you can forget she's sitting beside you, except for the sweet little inhale, exhale of her doggy breath. She's, in fact, not boring at all. She's a tender thing — polite and gentle and quiet. Sure, she'll bark at a squirrel, but who wouldn't?

Noodle's sweet disposition makes her the ideal companion for someone who needs to slow down their life for a while — which, as it turns out, was extremely fortunate. Very shortly after she brought Noodle home with her, Debbie was diagnosed with breast cancer. She went through surgery and treatment, which left her exhausted. During that time, sweet Noodle just curled up on the bed beside her and stayed there. Debbie swears that Noodle knew something was wrong, because she was quite fierce in her decision to stay by her side. She refused to move. She would not leave Debbie, not until she was well enough to move around.

Noodle was terrific company for someone in recovery like that; she just slept, nuzzled her snout into Debbie's neck and snoozed away the days until Debbie felt better. The company of a dog when you're bedbound is unspeakably lovely. It's healing and comforting and warm. The tiny snorting noises they make and the swelling of their chests as they breathe in and out beside you can be just enough to remind you why you want to return to your old life. The beat of their heart against your skin can be immensely soothing; the texture of their soft fur against your palm, powerfully calming and familiar.

Debbie's mum also discovered how lovely it was to have a buddy while recuperating. When she was about 79 years old, she broke her leg badly. It was a split in the thigh bone, so it was very painful and she required a full-leg cast. Debbie and her brother decided to get a carer to come by during the week to tend to their mama, but on weekends Debbie and her husband would scoop her up, drive her back home to their place and settle her into the comfiest armchair in the house. While they would fuss about, getting Debbie's mum in from the car, Noodle would pace frenetically back and forth, whimpering.

The moment Debbie's mum had snuggled into the armchair, Noodle would quieten down, bound over, gently jump onto her lap and place her head precisely where the break in her thigh bone was. She'd refuse to leave, just gingerly resting her little head where the pain was.

Before Debbie got too carried away declaring that she had some sort of magical genius dog who can diagnose breaks in human bone, she asked the vet why Noodle might be nestled so intently on that particular spot. The vet said that it's possible Noodle could feel the subtle movements of bone mending, the vibrations of a skeleton knitting itself back together and healing. It might feel quite nice for a creature who can detect that kind of movement. She might also have been picking up on the smell of stress hormones, the pained expression on Debbie's mother's face, or the change in behaviour.

Whatever the method of Noodle's empathy, it was deeply pleasant to have her be so attentive. Debbie's mother's blood pressure went down whenever she sat with Noodle. The act of stroking her soft, grey hair was soothing, which kept her calm and content. It changed the entire tone of her recovery period, giving her something to look forward to and to get used to doing.

After that time, it occurred to Debbie that perhaps Noodle the schnoodle could help other people who need company and comfort throughout illness. When on one of her regular walks with Noodle, she met a woman who had registered her schnauzer as a therapy dog, she decided to look into doing the same for Noodle. The schnoodle was duly tested to see whether she had the right temperament and liked interacting with strangers, and was then approved by the Mayhew Centre's TheraPaws team as a suitable candidate.

First, they were placed in the cancer research unit at a central London teaching hospital, where their patients ranged from an 18-year-old girl with bone cancer to elderly people with end-stage cancer, all undergoing complex experimental treatment.

While she was visiting, Noodle took part in a study. For a period of six weeks, everyone in the cancer care unit would have their blood pressure taken half an hour before Noodle's arrival. Everyone meant everyone: the nurses, the cleaners, the visitors. It included the patients who had opted to see therapy dogs and the patients who had opted not to. Then they'd all have their blood pressure taken again half an hour after Noodle had left and gone home with Debbie. Each time, everyone's blood pressure had gone down simply because they were in the presence of a dog. Even the people who didn't directly interact with Noodle. Even the people who'd asked not to touch Noodle. Even the people who'd just seen Noodle tending to someone else across the room.

It was gratifying for Debbie to have some sort of scientific conclusion to reference, when people asked her what help a schnoodle could possibly offer people in a time of such distress. She found that for every person who was thrilled by the idea of having a therapy dog visit, there was usually someone who found it immensely easy to be cynical about the efficacy of the program. She knew in her heart what good Noodle could do, but it's always nice to be backed up by research.

Debbie and Noodle spent two years at the cancer care unit, before being reassigned to a dementia care ward. Debbie learned about dementia from the Alzheimer's Society. She was taught how to speak to people who've forgotten most of their own lives because of dementia. She learned how to make conversation with someone who can't keep hold of their own memories, and how to safely get Noodle out of there if she needed to. She knew she'd probably be having a lot of the same conversations over and over — such is the nature of people who often forget what they've just said. She found out that she was meant to go along with whatever the person thought was happening, whether that meant pretending it was the 1950s or agreeing that they were entirely different people. You don't want to frighten someone out of their own perceived reality, or make them all too suddenly aware of what they've got wrong about themselves, or time, or place, or circumstance. So, tenderly, timidly, patiently, while Noodle provided solace and warmth, Debbie learned to be a comfort to fragile people herself, listening and chatting and sitting quietly by as someone cooed over her dog.

Many of the dementia patients Debbie visited would think that Noodle was their own dog, a dog they had left at home or a pet they had in previous decades, when they were younger. They'd greet Noodle with familiarity, as pleased as they would have been if a long-forgotten pet had simply bounded back into their lives.

One such time, a little old lady squealed with delight when she saw Noodle, declaring that it was her old dog come to visit. Noodle jumped up onto the bed, which she wouldn't ordinarily do (usually, she waits patiently by the bedside to be invited for a snuggle). This woman started telling stories about things she used to do with her dog, merrily chatting away, recalling the sorts of memories that were usually utterly lost to her. Eventually, she realised that Noodle wasn't her dog at all, but another, new, just as lovely companion. That didn't seem to worry her; she adapted quickly and continued to chat to her new friend.

Debbie made eye contact with the woman's son, who was sitting by her bed. She thought for a moment that he seemed annoyed. He didn't say anything, but he appeared to be just staring at his mother and this dog. Debbie wondered whether he might be thinking it was unhygienic for a dog to be sitting on his mother's bed. Feeling uncomfortable and wanting to alleviate any awkwardness, Debbie made her excuses to leave with Noodle. She apologised and left the woman with her son, promising to return sometime soon, but half-expecting to be asked not to.

Debbie had made it halfway down the hallway when the son came running after her. She presumed it was to confront her about having the dog on the bed, so she swiftly made her apologies and explained that ordinarily Noodle wouldn't get quite so close to the patients. As it turns out, the man was not appalled by canine hygiene standards at all. He was simply astonished, he explained, because that was the first time his mother had spoken in six weeks. In her state, she had recently become completely mute. He would still visit her, hoping she might be able to speak to him, to return, even briefly, to being the mother he'd known and loved his whole life. It wasn't until Noodle came sauntering into that room and plonked herself on his mother's lap that she felt able to utter a word. And not just a word, but a ream of excited memories. He was delighted, and shocked, and grateful. He pleaded with Debbie to please bring Noodle back to visit his mother as often as they could — and they did. Actually, they turned right around and went straight back into her room. 'Who is this?' said the woman, as though she'd never seen Noodle before.

And it's like that, working in a dementia unit. You watch as people disappear — from themselves, from their lives, from their families. You watch as this remorselessly cruel illness robs people of their memories and their identities. You watch as relatives and loved ones mourn the living, because their mother or their father or their spouse doesn't know who they are anymore. You learn that therapy dog visits are just as important for the visitors and bystanders as they are for the patients themselves, because sometimes, if they're lucky, when Noodle comes by, they get a small glimpse of the person their beloved used to be. It's an enormous relief for doctors and nurses, too, who spend their days tending to people who don't always know who they are or what's going on.

Debbie and Noodle have met some real characters in their years working in dementia wards. They met a woman in her seventies who'd worked her whole life as a vet. Everyone called her 'Doctor', in deference. When Noodle turned up, she immediately thought she had to do a medical check-up. 'Who's this?' she'd say. 'Let me take a look at her ... Yes, she seems to be in good health.' Debbie went along with it, because it let this woman step back into her old professional identity for a moment. Maybe it was comforting to feel important like that again, to be in charge, to do what you'd been trained to do. They also met a woman who became so enamoured with Noodle that she insisted on taking her by the lead and accompanying her on all her other visits.

Debbie and Noodle met an older gentleman who perpetually believed he was going to be picked up in half an hour. No matter what time of day it was, he'd have his shoes and his coat and his hat on, because he was convinced that his family were on their way to pick him up — always and forever 30 minutes away. He was stuck in this ready-to-go mentality for a long time, always waiting, never settling. The nurses would try to settle him for a moment at a time, convince him that he could sit while he waited, maybe watch a bit of telly, take his shoes off, relax. He'd get riled up and insist on standing up, waiting to leave this place. So when Noodle arrived, sometimes, for a while he'd agree to put his things down and play with the dog — for the eternal 30-minute period he thought he had left before people arrived to take him away. It didn't cure him; it didn't restore his sense of reality or time or life. It just gave him something to do while he waited, a living creature to pat and stroke and cuddle, a way to pass the time. Dogs can be an extremely effective distraction like that; a means of disrupting an otherwise seemingly endless day that stretches on without interruption or meaning. The nurses were always visibly relieved when Noodle showed up to visit this man, because they knew, even if it was just for a short while, that they'd have something to distract him. Sometimes that's all you can hope for: a distraction.

Debbie says that her years of visiting people with cancer and dementia, Noodle trotting along beside her, have been altruistic — but not exclusively so. Debbie gets a lot in return, too. She wanted to do something good for people who needed it, and it's given her enormous satisfaction to see the difference she and her canine companion can make in people's lives. It's rewarding for her, in that rather wonderful way exercising your compassion can be. She gets to meet terrific new people, make friends and listen to life stories. She gets to witness her dog making people smile and laugh. It brings her joy to be able to do that for strangers. Kindness feels nice when you practise it.

At times she's found it confronting and harrowing, too. She wonders what sort of lasting good she can possibly do for someone when that person is liable to forget the entire encounter they've had with her and Noodle. How do you help someone with dementia long term, when they can lose all memory of ever having met you, every time you see them? Is it worth giving someone a good day, if they're only going to forget it by supper time? Of course, it has to be. It's like our childhoods: we don't necessarily remember all of the details, but we know, somewhere in our psyche and our heart, whether we were happy. We might not be able to conjure the memory of every single time we spent with our parents and our siblings and our friends, but their positive presence in our lives meant something and it made us who we are as adults. For people with dementia, surely they have a sense of whether their life is a happy one, even if they can't hold onto the memory or the reality of every passing moment and hour? Contributing to the overall tone of someone's life, even if that experience disappears upon completion, has to be a powerful thing.

*

Debbie's account of Noodle helping people has now been corroborated by official research. In 2019, doctors at Middlesex University's Department of Mental Health and

Social Work published their assessment of the Mayhew Centre's TheraPaws program. Dr Briony Jain and her team set out to establish what sort of impact dog therapy was having on people who lived in care homes. They recruited residents, staff and volunteers from four care homes across London. Over a 12-week period in late 2018, they sent several researchers in once a week for 90 minutes to observe dogs visiting residents. They took detailed notes of what they thought the immediate short-term effects were. They ran focus groups with staff and volunteers at each of these establishments, to gather as many observations as they could and create a clear picture of what dogs might be able to do in such an environment. The residents they spent time with were aged between 57 and 103 years old, having stayed at a care home for between 0.1 and 24.9 months. The residents also filled in questionnaires about their happiness with the dog visits and their overall quality of life before and after.

The results were deeply pleasing — and absolutely corroborate Debbie's impressions of the good Noodle has been doing for her elderly companions. Researchers observed, and were told, that visiting dogs increased social interaction among the residents, prompting them to talk more than they would otherwise to each other, the staff members who care for them, and the volunteers who bring their dogs in. Seeing a dog — even for people who declared themselves cat people — was a catalyst for conversation and an enabler of social interaction that simply wouldn't have happened otherwise. The animals also provided companionship for these elderly residents, many of whom live incredibly isolated lives.

The academics who spent time in these care homes also found that a visit from a dog could unlock memories and emotions in the residents, just like Debbie said. Staff and volunteers reported that people would look at a dog and suddenly remember all sorts of lovely things about former pets, people they'd known or places they'd been in their lives. They'd share these memories — even the people who were usually quiet — with whoever was present. These are things they wouldn't have thought about otherwise; stories that would have gone untold.

Staff members also spoke about the relationships they noticed forming because of the dog's presence. People would become talkative and start to trust the volunteers who brought them a dog to touch and snuggle. They'd speak, where otherwise they may have been mute or uncommunicative. Staff and volunteers believe that these dogs significantly increase the overall quality of life for people they visit in care homes — and I find that utterly unsurprising.

The majority of residents who filled in a questionnaire about dog visits ticked the box for 'very much' enjoying it and would like to have more frequent visits. Without exception, the carers described a positive effect on the environment at their homes, and said the general lift in mood could last hours after a dog had left. It's a resounding confirmation of what we already thought we knew about these programs: that the presence of dogs in a care home is an overwhelmingly lovely, often bafflingly powerful force for good.

By 2050, adults over the age of 60 will likely make up 25 per cent of the national population in many countries around the world. Today, 125 million people are over the age of 80, but by 2050 that number will be 434 million across the planet (with 120 million in China alone). We are going to have to find ways to care for these people, but also to make them feel tended to, loved and human. In the UK, there are 400,000 people currently living in care homes. There are 200,000 people in Australian care homes and more than 1.5 million in America. We are looking at a future in which we have to care for a rapidly expanding older generation urgently and sensitively.

It is imperative that we find cost-effective, simple ways to improve these people's lives. We now know that spending time with a dog does exactly that, so it would be smart to implement more animal therapy programs across the world's care homes. It is scientifically evidenced how wonderful a dog visit can be for an older person, whether they have a dementia diagnosis or not. It makes them feel comforted and safe and happy — which is a true gift in such a place.

My grandmother spent the final decade of her life begging not to be put in a care home. When she was eventually admitted to one, she befriended a filthy little myna bird who flew in her window and stole her toast every morning. She defied her nurse's request that she shut the window to prevent him from coming in, and delighted in watching him sit on the end of her bed, quite pleased with himself for scavenging a piece of bread slathered in marmalade.

My darling grandma — a lifelong dog person, and the only other person I've ever known who was as devoted to her pets as I am — had to leave her dog, Archie, with her son when she went into a home, so she craved animal attention in any form. She would have jumped out of her reclining armchair, if she had been able to, when a golden retriever used to drop by for visits, so desperate was she to touch and smell and dote on a dog again. It was a profound joy for her, just to be in the presence of an animal. Her sweet, soft face would light up and she'd talk about it for the rest of the day. So when researchers say that dogs can improve the overall quality of someone's life, I absolutely, wholeheartedly believe them. My grandmother would have enthusiastically endorsed programs like this.

Many years before my grandma ended up in a home because she could no longer care for herself, she was in hospital recovering from an operation. She was frail and miserable, mostly because she had to be away from her dog. My mum and I snuck him in to cheer her up one day, and I genuinely believe that that one appearance from him motivated her to stay alive, heal and get healthy enough to be released and go home. Back at home, she would feed him toast, let him rest on what used to be my papa's armchair, and fall asleep each night with his little body tucked into the small of her back. That dog kept her alive longer than she would have been otherwise, I just know it. He was one of the great loves of her life.

I think of her now and know what tremendous joy she would have felt, seeing a dog like Noodle come into her room. She was utterly miserable in a care home, her misery only relieved by a daily visit from my mother, who often came bearing fresh mango as a treat. That's what dogs can do, too; they can provide warmth and compassion and attention, the likes of which old people in care homes usually do not see often enough.

If I can find the time, one day I'd like to volunteer in a care home with my dog. It would be a privilege to speak to the elderly people who live there. It would be a joy to know that my beloved pet could make a difference, even a small one, to someone's day. That's all we can hope for and that's all we can do: look for ways to brighten people's lives when they're nearing the end of their time on Earth. Dogs are the most life-brightening presence I can imagine. Take them to visit our old folks. Take them, for that matter, to anyone who might like a visit from one.

CONCLUSION

Good dogs are the greatest creatures we have

EVERY DOG OWNER BELIEVES that their hairy friend is the best dog in the world. We are all correct. I happen to think that Bert, my shih tzu, is the greatest animal who ever lived, wagged and snored. He's a sweet, stubborn nugget of a dog, and he makes my life better every single day. He is asleep beside me right now, snoring heartily and occasionally rolling his eyes around in their sockets in his slumber. He is one of the great loves of my life, and I do not appreciate ever having to be apart from him. Bert's predecessor, Lady (Beyoncé) Fluffington, still has part of my heart, too. She was a precious treasure, who could nevertheless fart and snore better than just about anyone. The dogs I've adopted as an adult have become supremely important to me. I am ridiculous in my commitment to these creatures. I know that; don't think I'm oblivious. I can only hope it's endearing.

I once saw an elderly woman in the park, shrugged into several cardigans, walking seven dogs of different sizes. Two of them were in prams, the rest were at the ends of different-coloured leads. I know now, as I knew then, that this is just a glimpse into my future. I am simply destined to surround myself with as many dogs as I can, for as long as I may live. Sceptics might think me mad, but what if my love of dogs actually keeps me alive longer than I would otherwise have lived? Who's laughing then?

For many years we've had evidence that suggests dogs are good for human health. We know that they reduce our blood pressure, slow our heart rate and boost our immune system. We know this can alleviate emotional states like anxiety, depression and loneliness. We know dogs coax us into regular physical activity outside, in nature, which is immeasurably good for us. Now, though, we have an even clearer idea of just how good pet companionship is for us. Two separate studies came out towards the end of 2019 that suggest living with a dog can actually extend the length of time we live.

The first study, by Carolyn Kramer and her team at the University of Toronto, evaluated ten studies dating back more than five decades and including 3.8 million people. They compared people who live with a dog to those who do not, and found that dog owners have a 24 per cent lower risk of dying, from any cause, over a ten-year period. When they looked at these results for people who had lived through a heart attack, the benefits of dog ownership were even more pronounced. People who lived with a dog after their heart attack had a 65 per cent lower risk of dying.

The second study, by Tove Fall and her team at Uppsala University in Sweden, looked again at the value of cohabiting with a dog for people who have had a heart attack or a stroke. They identified 335,000 patients who'd suffered one of those attacks between the years 2000 and 2012, five per cent of whom were dog owners. Among people who'd had a heart attack, their risk of dying was 33 per cent lower if they owned a dog. For those who had a stroke, the risk of dying was 27 per cent lower if they lived with a dog, compared to people who live alone. Researchers on this study noted that dog owners tend to be more physically active, which of course probably has a decent impact on their longevity. Surely, too, the stress relief provided by a dog contributes to our durability as people.

We know, too, that dogs show us what it is to love and be loved. We cherish and adore our slobbery companions.

Perhaps not right at the moment they passionately vomit on us or when they destroy our favourite pair of shoes, but most of the time there's a very precious love between a human and their dog. I see it every day, with my Bert. I see it with my dad and step-mum's miraculous dogs, Molly the enormous golden retriever and Agnes the refined standard poodle. I see it walking down the street, chatting away to other people on the tall end of the lead. I see it, too, in the eyes of strangers when my boyfriend boards a bus wearing Bert strapped into a purpose-built turquoise backpack. Some people don't care for dogs, sure. Some people are allergic, or indifferent, or unamused, or unable to interact with dogs for cultural reasons. But millions and millions of people do care for dogs, very much — and they know how special it can be to have one, maybe two, perhaps five, in your life. Dogs are darling, sweet creatures who deserve to be doted on, walked, snuggled and given treats.

For many thousands of years, dogs have been important to humankind. They started out as our allies, helping us find food and stay safe. Over the centuries we've bred them to accentuate their best traits: loyalty, friendliness and cuteness. Some of that breeding has been irresponsible and now we have certain types of dogs with serious health problems.

I would personally like to see less breeding of dogs in general, especially when it's for aesthetic purposes. If you're ever thinking of getting a pet dog, I'd urge you wholeheartedly to visit a rescue shelter. There are so many dogs on this planet right now who need loving homes. I would beg you, also, to care for that dog as long as you possibly can. To keep them safe. To make them feel loved. To treat them and walk them and cuddle them. To behave as though you are lucky to have them, because you are.

The whole point of this book has been, really, to celebrate how good dogs are. 'How good are dogs?' I say, regularly, to the people in my life. 'Have you met Bert?' I say, any chance I can get. 'Do you think he might be the best boy who ever lived?' I believed dogs were amazing before I started writing — I have believed it all my life — and now I believe it even more emphatically.

Good dogs are the greatest creatures we have, bless them. Often kinder and more generous with their affection than human beings. Often smarter and simpler and freer. Often more endearing, more effusive and more affectionate than we all know how to be. We would, most of us, do well to emulate dogs, for their enthusiasm and their optimism and their courage. They are loyal and they are good. They live in hope, whether it's hoping for a treat or hoping for a walk or hoping for a pat. Hope is one of our greatest states as living creatures, and they've mastered it.

Dogs so often make us the gentlest versions of ourselves, too, ready for a snuggle, or a play, or an act of kindness. As we now know, dogs actively make our lives better. They make us stronger, they make us healthier, they make us happier. They change our lives, they improve our lives, and, yes, in some cases they save our lives.

It has been a profound privilege to meet all the dogs you've read about in these pages. Of course, first, we had my Bert. He is often asleep, but even then he's adding to my life, murmuring and swiping his paws through the air as he dreams of cats and cheese. He remains one of the greatest sources of joy in my life. Each day, he finds a way to make me appreciate being in his company. Even when he steals my socks, or throws up on my lap, or barks for no discernible reason at 3 am, I still love him. I could not love him more if I tried. He is just so good, I refuse to be ashamed that I speak to him every day, sometimes in the presence of other human beings, but often when we're on our own. I read a study once that said people who speak to their pets out loud are actually smarter, and I stand by that in my defence forever more.

Since writing so effusively about my Bert, I have started to appreciate him even more, if that's possible. If I'm anxious or nervous or scared, I remember that he can help me and I go to him for comfort. If anyone who comes to my home feels those things, I urge them to sit with Bert for a moment or I simply place him on their lap, knowing he will settle in for a much-needed snuggle. I basically prescribe his affection to people I love, and rely on him to lift my mood when it dips. I also think about how it is my responsibility to give him a good, interesting, safe, happy life, and I try to do that as much as I can. He lives well. I wish he could read what I've written about him here, I wish he could know how much of a difference he makes to my life. Alas, I will have to make do with giving him extra treats for a reason he will not understand but certainly not object to.

I marvel, now, at the ways dogs can affect human beings. How Bert affects me. He is, perhaps ridiculously, one of my most reliable ways of knowing and liking who I am. With him, I am gentle and tender and patient; I care and I like how that feels. Sometimes I think about the fact that he is mortal, and I ache with that knowledge because I cannot think of my life without him. It will be my great honour to care for him as long as I can.

We have a happy life together, our little family. He makes my relationship with my boyfriend better all the time, because it is a powerfully bonding activity, to care for a small, stout living creature. He is also dear, now, to the rest of my human family, the friends who have had the pleasure of making his acquaintance and the many strangers who follow his escapades on Instagram. Adopting him is one of the proudest achievements of my life, and I really mean that. We have been able to give this wonky-eyed, fluffy-bottomed, snub-snouted creature a safe, enthusiastically loving home. In exchange, he gives us love and affection and solace and amusement and warmth and comfort and even something to live for, when it's required. He is a special little guy.

And then ... the others! Missy the autism support pug. Echo the valiant therapy labrador. Pip the remarkable diabetic alert dog. Jingles the lively prison pup. Poppi the gorgeous guide dog. Mya the gallant border collie spaniel cross. Gwen the elegant court companion. Jack the sensitive border terrier. Teddy the brave hospital dog. Noodle the compassionate schnoodle.

We have spent time with 11 remarkable dogs. All of them sweet and patient and adorable. All of them living with wonderful, kind human beings. I have travelled across the world to meet these dogs and their people — and it has been my overwhelming pleasure. If I thought dogs were good before I set out, I think it more certainly than ever before now. I have seen for myself how powerfully dogs can change human lives. I have seen them cheer and cajole and snuggle. I have seen them work and listen and support. I have seen them give human beings a reason to live. It has been deeply moving. I have cried, I have laughed. I have been slobbered on, I have been greeted with wagging tails.

I have never been more sure that our future together, human and dog, can only get better. The more acceptable it becomes to have our dogs in public spaces with us, the more normal it becomes to train a dog to assist someone, and the more funding we give to the right programs, the better that relationship can be. I want to live in a world where it's entirely commonplace to see dogs in cafés, courts, hospitals, schools, prisons and offices. I want to live in a world where we don't challenge a person's right to take their dog anywhere.

I truly believe we are discovering again and again how powerfully wonderful and sometimes even vital dogs can be — and I'd like to think we will make the most of that relationship. We know now that dogs can dramatically improve human lives, whether they were simply born sweet, slobbery angels or because we train them specifically to help us. I hope we will continue to learn, continue to rescue dogs and, in turn, continue to be changed by them ourselves.

People and our canine companions. Long may we snuggle.

Acknowledgements

THANK YOU, FIRST, TO the wonderful human beings who spoke to me about their dogs for this book. To Jill, Cody, Aideen, Geraldine, Shirley, Katie, Cassandra, Barry, Mark, Julie, Casey, Ness, Andy, Debbie and Niamh: thank you. Thank you for inviting me into your life, even for an afternoon. Thank you for being so generous with your stories. Thank you for allowing me to pat your gorgeous animals. I hope you will continue to send me dog photos.

Thank you, obviously, to my publisher, Catherine Milne. You always like my dog's Instagram posts and you've brought that enthusiasm over to this book. I adore working with you and hope we can do it again. Thank you also to the whole team at HarperCollins – you made it such a pleasure to put this book together.

Thank you to my agent, Martin Redfern. You believed in this mad book from the first time I mentioned it to you and you fought valiantly for it. Thank you to Diane Banks and the team at Northbank Talent for looking out for me.

Thank you to my much adored family and friends: for the love, the support, the WhatsApp messages. I never lose sight, not for a day, of how lucky I am to have you in my life.

Thank you, thank you, thank you to my darling Jono. You are handsome and patient and gentle. I am forever thankful that you came into my life and very pleased that you happen to have superb proofreading skills. You helped make this a better book and I hope you will always read what I write so thoughtfully.

And lastly, to my Bertie. I know you can't read all the effusive words I've written about you, including these, but I cherish your sweet little face every day. You are the goodest boy of all.

Also by Kate Leaver

THE FRIENDSHIP CURE:

The Art of Friendship and Why it Matters More Than Ever

The basic compulsion to make friends is in our DNA; we've evolved chimp-like, to seek out connection with others. We move through life in packs and friendship circles and yet we are stuck in the greatest loneliness epidemic of our time. It's killing us, making us miserable and causing a public health crisis. But what if friendship is the solution, not the distraction?

Kate Leaver believes that friendship is the essential cure for the modern malaise of solitude, ignorance, ill health and angst. If we only treated camaraderie as a social priority, it could affect everything from our physical health and emotional well-being to our capacity to find a home, keep a job, get married, stay married, succeed, feed and understand ourselves.

In this book, a witty, smart, thought-provoking and appealing exploration of friendship, she meets scientists, speaks to old friends, finds extraordinary stories and uncovers research to look at what friendship is, how to keep it, why we need it and what we can do to get the most from it — and how we might change the world if we value it properly.